Quick and Easy Texas Hold'em

Quick and Easy
Texas Hold'em

Learn to Play Poker's Most Popular Game

NEIL D. MYERS

LYLE STUART
KENSINGTON PUBLISHING CORP.
WWW.KENSINGTONBOOKS.COM

LYLE STUART BOOKS are published by

Kensington Publishing Corp.
850 Third Avenue
New York, NY 10022

Playing cards courtesy of U.S. Playing Card Company

All Kensington titles, imprints, and distributed lines are available at special quantity discounts for bulk purchases for sales promotions, premiums, fund-raising, educational or institutional use. Special book excerpts or customized printings can also be created to fit specific needs. For details, write or phone the office of the Kensington special sales manager: Kensington Publishing Corp., 850 Third Avenue, New York, NY 10022, attn: Special Sales Department; phone: 1-800-221-2647.

Lyle Stuart is a trademark of Kensington Publishing Corp.

First printing: August 2005

10 9 8 7 6 5 4 3 2 1

Printed in the United States of America

ISBN 0-8184-0654-3

To my wife, Susan, who is a much better writer than me. Without your help, love, support, and encouragement (and your constant eye on my grammar), this book would never have been written.

Contents

Acknowledgments

Like a speech at the Oscars, one invariably feels that someone important has been missed when an acknowledgment is penned, so sorry if I have by mistake. Here goes!

I would like to thank my editor at Citadel, Richard Ember, as well as the editor-in-chief, Gene Brissey, and all the Citadel and Kensington staff from all departments who have helped pull this together. I would especially like to thank Bruce Bender, who was prepared to give a new author with a good idea a chance.

I wish to thank the U.S. Playing Card Company, Inc., for their kind permission in granting me the use of their "Bee" brand playing cards in the DVD and for allowing us to use the card images throughout the text.

Thank you John Seymour at www.pokershoppe.com for the use of the poker table in the DVD and for supplying us with chips. I also wish to thank Jim Christina at Foxwoods Casino in Connecticut for putting me in touch with our dealer on the DVD, Dan Carpenter. Thanks Jim and Dan.

Thanks to Howard Bond, Josh Condon, Matt Guarino, Brad Reeves, Helen Resseguie, Ray Siler, Rob Taschler, Jennifer Vendettuoli and of course my wife, Susan Myers, who were all willing to give up a Sunday to film a poker DVD. The DVD could not have been made without the sterling advice and skill of Gene Simco and his staff, and I must thank Heather Simco for allowing me the use of her house and her husband just days after the birth of their first child!

Last but not least, all the clubs, casinos, card rooms and especially the players who have allowed me to hone my poker skills, often at their (the players') expense: Thanks, guys!

Introduction

THIS PART OF the book is supposed to tell you something about me and why on earth you should listen to anything I have to say about **poker**. So in respect of that tradition, sit down, grab a snack or a warm beverage, and let me tell you who I am and how I became interested in poker and, anyway, who on earth am *I* to tell *you* how to play poker?

Well let me tell you first who I am *not*. I am *not*, at least as I write this, a poker world champion, nor have I won a succession of large **tournaments**, nor have I been playing poker for fifty years. In fact I am pretty much like *you*. You see, the last person you want to teach you poker is a world champion or someone who has played for fifty years. Why? Well, because their experiences are so different from yours, playing as you will in small low-**limit** cash games, that they might as well be on a different planet.

Top poker players are normally playing in tournaments against other top players, where they stand to make hundreds of thousands and sometimes millions of dollars, or they are playing cash games for sums equal to what many of us earn in a year. They live in a different world. Most of us will never have the experience of pushing $100,000 into a **pot** to **see** the **Turn** of a card. Most of us do not have the emotional makeup or mental skill to play in this world, although many of us might fantasize about it in the same way that we may have wished as children to play in a World Series or represent our country at the Olympics.

Now what we want to do is play in a game for modest stakes, win more than we lose, and have some fun. This is what this book is about, and here I can claim some expertise because for three years I made a part of my income playing in these types of games and beating them week in week out, month after month, year after year and because I still beat these games today.

I began playing poker because I needed the money. I needed to supplement my income, and I needed to learn and learn fast how to beat the low-limit game consistently. The low-limit game is *not* like the high-limit game. Not at all. It is as different from high-limit as college baseball is from major league baseball. Players in high-limit games often do badly in low-limit games. When watching the *World Series of Poker*, I happened to see on TV someone who I used to play with in New York. I beat him regularly, even though he was, and is, a better player than I was! How? He never understood the low-limit game. He would try to make complex plays against poor players. He would get frustrated and emotional about others' bad play. He does very well at higher limits, and his game and temperament is much more suited to the roller-coaster world of high-limit and tournament play than the low-limit world, where his opportunity to make daring and sophisticated plays is very limited.

So here is the primary reason you should pay attention to my advice: *It's because I have played thousands of hours of low-limit* Texas Hold'em, *both live and over the Internet, and consistently beaten the games I have played in.*

When it comes to this game, quite simply, I know what I am talking about. You will have to take nothing on faith in this book. I will explain to you exactly why I recommend each move and play. I know, not because I am a genius or an original thinker, but because I have studied, played, thought, reflected, sought advice from experts, studied and played, and played and played. In low-limit Hold'em, for thousands of hours, I have distilled the essentials and presented them here, for your edification and enjoyment. So you can play poker, learn it quickly and easily, and have *fun*. I am no more intelligent or special than you are. *You* can become an excellent Hold'em player if you stand on the shoulders of good players and take their advice. It's all here in this book. With far less time and study than was necessary for me, you can quickly become a very strong player, and many of you will become better players than me. Think of me as your poker coach, whose job is to help you build solid foundations for your game. But please don't call me "Coach": it makes me feel like a bus.

So how did I begin this poker odyssey? Well, from the time of my late teens, I was intrigued by gambling. When I was seventeen, I ran across the writings of the French philosopher René Descartes. I was intrigued to discover that not only was he a philosopher and soldier, but he made a goodly part of his income from games of chance. Being a brilliant mathematician, he worked out that certain games in his day were very beatable if you understood the mathematics of the game. He played them and seemed to have won enough to philosophize about life at some leisure. His gambling buddies must have found that a real pain, but he had his mind on higher things. He made money beating beatable games. That sounded like fun.

At about this time I discovered that one Richard Nixon, who some of you may know, played poker as a young naval officer, well enough to win a substantial stake, which he used to partially fund his first political campaign. Several other former presidents seemed to know how to **play** a decent hand of poker too. I found this fascinating.

In London (I am a Brit), when I was eighteen, I determined to see if there were beatable casino games. My conclusions were depressing: while there were many system peddlers, none seemed capable of beating the games of chance because the **house** always stacked the **odds** in its favor. Roulette was unbeatable, unless you could find a biased table, despite the innumerable number of "system" players who seemed to lose their money trying to prove otherwise. Punto Banco or Baccarat seemed possibly beatable, but nobody knew for sure. Sports handicapping was beatable, but demanded lots of study, great information, and a **bankroll** sufficient to withstand large swings. Craps was fun but not beatable long term and not played too much in the United Kingdom.

That left Blackjack. Definitely beatable, as at times the odds favored the player, and so I experimented with card counting. I won a little money but what hard work. You had to have immense concentration and the multideck games with shallow penetration shuffles and unfavorable rules made the game unbeatable for all intents and purpose. No good poker games were available in the United Kingdom, and anyway how would I learn that stuff?

Move forward twelve years. I find myself in New York working as a visa slave. That is being sponsored by a company to work in the United States, but for a wage far less than a U.S. citizen would make for the same job. How to supplement my meager income with an activity that was fun and still be able to pay New York prices. I looked again at Blackjack. Atlantic City casinos were big but offered rules almost as unfavorable as the United Kingdom. Then I remembered Nixon (who could ever forget him?) and started to look for poker books. I found my first. Knowing nothing about the game, I taught myself. My first learning volume was hopelessly out of date and talked mostly about Five-Card Draw as if it were the only game in town. I persevered. I organized a nickel and dime poker night for a few friends and found I did quite well. I think I won two bucks! Could the game be beaten? Could I make some money on the side? Yes and Yes. Poker is essentially a game of skill. I just had to become good at it and find players worse than I was who would play for money!

Now as my wife will tell you, much to her annoyance sometimes, when I really want to know something, I become obsessed with it for as long as I feel it takes to overcome it, or at least to satisfy my curiosity; so it became with poker. I searched for books. Poker books, unlike today, were scarce. I went to a specialist gambling shop in Manhattan seeking advice on poker books. The assistant sagely pointed out a few volumes, which I later learned were pretty rotten books. Sensing I was a complete beginner, one assistant waxed lyrical about how his best casino game was Five-Card **Stud** that he had played in "AC" just last week. What a crock! When he was telling me this, no casino in Atlantic City had probably **spread** Five-Card Stud for twenty years.

Then I discovered Hold'em—the game of the world champions. The "Cadillac" of poker as **Doyle Brunson** once referred to the **no-limit** game. I owe a great debt to writers like Lee Jones, David Sklansky, Mason Malmuth, and Ray Zee. Their books opened my eyes to real poker and its possibilities. I read voraciously everything they wrote. I bought a poker program from Wilson software and played against it for hours and hours and hours, until I was following the correct play actions almost reflexively. I was beating the computer players all the time. I was ready for the casino! I thought.

A short while later I find myself in the palace of gaudiness: the Trump Taj Mahal in Atlantic City. Overcome by it size and over-the-top splendor, I find my way to the poker room, and after a long wait and a perusal of the **tables**, I buy into a $2–$4 Hold'em game for $100. The game seems to move fast. All the players seem confident and know what they are doing. Perhaps I am not as good as I thought. I fold hand after hand. At last, **pocket** kings, and almost by reflex I say "**raise**." My English accent is mildly mocked, but I care not. Then there were two **callers**, a raise, and a **re-raise**. My goodness, I think, they must both have pocket kings, but slightly afraid, I **call**. The **Flop**, I do not remember, but I remember my kings look good. I bet out, and I am raised again! I nervously call. Three players left. The **Turn** comes, I **check**. One player bets, one folds, I call. The **River** brings a jack. I am confused. I check, the other player bets confidently and stares at me. Does he have **two pair**? An **overpair**? My heart is beating faster. I call, expecting the worst, but feeling somehow I should call, as there is no ace out. He proudly turns over a jack and nine. Still confused I turn over my kings. Have I missed something? "Good hand," he barks, and I realize I have won all those **chips** in the middle. I quickly drag them in and start to pile them up. I have begun playing casino poker.

I remember what it was like to be confused and nervous in a casino. Like you, I know what it is like to learn a card game from books as an adult, not playing as a kid or in dorm rooms or on the road as a professional card player. I remember thinking that everyone was better than I was and that I would probably never play well. I was wrong. Good books, computer play, and playing against opponents who were at about my level turned me into a good player. After a few months, I realized that years of experience did not, in itself, make players any good if they did not study or were not "naturals."

I continued to play each weekend and then in some of the semi-legal poker clubs of New York. I did not win all the time, but I slowly and steadily increased my poker bankroll as my skills improved. Finally, I was playing poker in clubs in New York most evenings and in Atlantic City on the weekends. I was not making a lot at poker but I was playing over thirty hours a week and averaging about $12–$15 an hour, in $4–$8 and $5–$10 games, sometimes $10–$20. Those monthly boosts of $1,000 to $1,800 or so were not a fortune, but they provided a nice chunk of pocket money and payed some bills. I did not feel the need to move up. I was doing quite nicely, and poker became my second job. I ran into some interesting and bizarre characters around the tables, some nasty and some very personable and interesting. I played some tournaments. I did quite well winning a couple and getting placed. I had become a poker player.

Today, I still play in the casinos and on the Internet. You might see me around the tables, and who knows, I might get lucky in one of those televised tournaments. Essentially, though, I now play poker for fun, knowing that I can still make a modest living at the low-limit and mid-limit games if I choose, but preferring instead to play poker for fun and a little money and make my living doing other things.

So that is a little about me. Not very mysterious and no great heroics. Just an ordinary guy, fascinated by poker and wanting to have some fun. Read this book, follow its suggestions, have a good time, and maybe win some money too. Go get 'em, tiger!*

Who This Book Is For

I have always found it useful, when considering the purchase of a new book, to know right away if the author intended it for someone like me. So in answer to that question, if you are in one or more of the following categories, you will benefit from reading, studying, and applying the contents of this book:

---

* My aim is to be gender neutral, so I have used the third-person masculine throughout, well aware that poker players are also feminine.

1. *Complete beginners:* If you have never played any form of poker before, fear not. The rudiments of the game are laid out in the following pages. Before I learned Hold'em, I only played a little bit of Five-Card Draw for *very* low stakes. You don't have to learn another poker style before becoming proficient at Texas Hold'em. This volume will prove an ideal primer.

2. *Players who have played a little poker:* If you have played some poker of any type, either as a youth or in college or with friends or family, and want to learn about this most popular and exciting form of poker, you will find in this book everything you need to become a good player. You will learn what real poker players need to know and how the casino game differs from a home game. You will learn what makes Texas Hold'em different from other poker games and why it is so much fun to play. You will learn a conservative but winning method of play.

3. *Players who have played another form of poker and wish to learn Texas Hold'em:* You play other styles of poker—perhaps quite well—but have not yet tried Texas Hold'em. This may be because up to now you have only played say **Seven-Card Stud** and have decided to expand your poker horizons. This book will be very valuable because it will stop you from making the common mistakes that Stud players make when they try Hold'em for the first time. You will learn what makes **community card** poker unique and how card values and starting hands are different from those of other poker games. You will learn a solid style of play that you can use as the foundation for going onto bigger games if you wish.

4. *Players who have played some Texas Hold'em but are losing consistently:* You have the bug. You somehow learned and began playing Texas Hold'em, but your game is full of holes. You are losing money and not having fun doing so; other players are beating you up at the table and you want it to stop. This book will turn you from a 98-pound poker weakling into a he-man (or woman) at the

low-limit tables. You will no longer have sand kicked in your face! If you follow this book carefully, you will realize why you have been losing, and you will know exactly what to do about it. You will realize that poker is a game of skill, not chance, and that you can become a skillful player by following the methods I describe.

5. *Players who want to play casino poker for the first time:* You've seen it on TV; your friends are doing it; your neighbors are at it; and your work colleagues are doing it—even your mother-in-law—they're going off to the casino to play poker! Are you feeling left out? Well, now you can join in the fun because this book will show you everything you need to know to play poker in a casino or public card room. By using this book, you will save years gaining painful "experience" and save a ton of money that is normally lost by novices when they play in card rooms for the first time. You will no longer feel overwhelmed, and by studying and applying the methods in this book, you will have a far more enjoyable time when at a casino than playing slots, roulette, or Blackjack. You won't be playing an unbeatable game against the house, but playing a game of skill against other players. By reading and following my methods, you will be able to dominate most low-limit games.

6. *Higher-stakes players who wish to learn about low-limit Texas Hold'em:* If you play mid- or higher-stakes poker in another game, you may decide to try your hand at Hold'em. This book will explain why you play the low-limit game differently from the mid- and high-limit games if you want to win. It also shows why you may prefer at times to play in lower-limit games. It may even tell you things you never knew or remind you of things you did, but have since forgotten.

7. *The intellectually curious:* Are you the type who is fascinated by all human endeavors? Then for goodness sake, pick up another book and stop reading about poker, unless you intend to play! What are

you, nuts? Read about something else like philosophy, history, ethics, or stamp collecting. This book is for people who want to play!

How to Use This Book and How It Will Benefit You

This book is very straightforward to use. If you have never played Hold'em poker before, just read the book straight through. Each topic is covered in the order you need to first learn and then to play the game well. I describe exactly what you need to know at each stage of the hand, how to analyze the game and other players, how much money you will need to play, and what sort of games gives you the best chance to win.

If you have played poker before, but not Texas Hold'em, read all the chapters. If you can play Texas Hold'em and are sure that you know the rules and play of the hand, then you can skip the chapters that describe this. However, whatever you think you know about the game, unless you are a consistent winner, I recommend that you read the whole book and do not skip chapters. Many of the earlier chapters contain a number of key concepts that you will need to know and understand to play solid Hold'em—so skip them at your peril!

You must read, learn, and memorize the starting hands. There is no way around this. I have avoided the use of charts and tables. Many people, me included, find this a cumbersome way to learn this information. Instead, I've explained and summarized the types of starting hands you can play from different **positions**, and I also explain why this is so. Position and starting hand choices are inextricably linked, and if you learn them together, you are much more likely to remember *and* understand why you are making the plays I suggest. Unlike some poker writers, I have been somewhat conservative in the range and number of recommended starting hands. I have deliberately avoided suggesting those starting hands that are likely to mean that you will be faced with complex decisions later in the hand. It is true that more skilled players can play a larger range of starting hands, but they do not always increase their playing advantage by as much as they be-lieve by doing so. In fact, playing too many starting hands is one of the biggest reasons why players lose money at Texas Hold'em. By follow-ing my recommendations, you will avoid this error.

After starting hands in chapter 5, the next, and possibly most im-portant (and certainly the longest), chapter, chapter 6, deals with play on the Flop. You should read and study this over and over again. I have laid it out so that it covers just about every poker decision you will face. It requires careful and repeated study. This chapter not only contains many important concepts, but it will teach you how to think about different poker scenarios, when you hold just about any play-able hand. It will also save you money by showing you which hands are just about *unplayable*. If you follow the recommendations in the book, you will be able to do well in just about any low-limit game.

If you have never played poker in a casino or public card room, I urge you to read about what to expect when you do. It is nothing like a home game. It does not have **wild cards** or dealer's choice or eccen-tric rules. Players will be better and the game will move much faster. If you play in a casino without reading a book like this, you will feel overwhelmed and outclassed by the unfamiliar atmosphere. Follow-ing the guidelines I have laid out will make it an enjoyable and excit-ing experience instead.

This brings me to the main point of this book: this book is not about becoming a professional player. Other books have covered this ground, in many cases very well. This book is aimed at recreational players who may play regularly—but not necessarily every day—and play to have *fun*. They are playing primarily for enjoyment. They are not play-ing to pay the bills or aiming to become world champions, but to have an enjoyable time on weekends and on vacation or whenever else they choose to play. When you become a good poker player, you will be having more fun than anybody else will in the casino. You will be playing against other players, not the house—against whom you can hardly ever win if you play other games—and yet you will have lively social interaction, some good conversations, an intellectual challenge, and an opportunity to experience the thrills of the game of poker. You will win because of skill. Ultimately, poker is a game of skill. You will have fun because you'll know what you're doing and will have a structured, orderly approach. You will be a skilled player. Real fun in poker comes from winning and improving your skills and from learning to recognize a sound bet—one where *you* have the advantage. If poker is, for you, something that can only be enjoyed if you play with wild and reckless abandon and "gamble it up," this book and its methods are not for you. In fact, poker is not for you, not unless you have very deep pockets.

So dive in and remember: it's about having *fun*, because if you're not having fun in poker, then you should spend your leisure time on something else. Life is too varied, wonderful, and short to do otherwise.

PART ONE

Basic Concepts

CHAPTER ONE

Why Play Texas Hold'em?

S O YOU'VE DECIDED to take the plunge. You have made the commitment to read a book so you can come to the casino to play "real" poker. If you've ever gazed across a poker room at a midsize or large casino, you may find yourself bewildered at the array of poker games offered. They all seem to have exotic and confusing names to boot such as Omaha High, Omaha Hi-Low Split (Eights or better that is!), and Seven-Card Stud. At a larger casino you may even find the odd game of Five-Card Draw, Low Ball, or Crazy Pineapple. Many casinos will offer the more popular games in Pot-Limit or even No-Limit forms. Ignore 'em all! Run to the limit Texas Hold'em (I'll call it Hold'em from now on, for short) tables, and at least for now (maybe forever), pretend the rest don't exist. Your poker universe should consist of **limit Hold'em** and only limit Hold'em. If you need convincing, here are twelve reasons why you should play limit Hold'em.

1. *It gives you the best chance of a decent win without too much risk.* The correct way to assess risk in a poker game is through a statistical measure known as the *standard deviation*. You won't need to know too much about that just now and maybe not ever. Basically, it's a measure of short-term luck in a game. Watch out, I'm about to go mildly technical on you! The poorer the relationship between the win rate (**expectation**) and the standard deviation, the greater the

fluctuation; in other words, how badly you can run. In Hold'em this relationship is very good. If you play correctly, you can win more money for less risk.

Practically, this means that you can bring less cash to the table for a given limit than just about any other form of poker. You can also play more safely at a higher limit, if you choose to. It also means that you have less likelihood of busting your bankroll— never a pleasant experience.

2. *It rewards a disciplined, conservative approach.* The approach to Hold'em described in this book is solid: **tight** but **aggressive** at the right time. Since you probably are a new player, the strategy that I describe and you will apply is somewhat conservative. What does that mean to you? *It means that if you follow it, you may not win as much as a more skillful player in the same game, but you can relax because you will put little money at risk and you will often walk away with a nice win.* I maintain that it is easier to learn a sound, conservative, money-winning approach in Hold'em than in any other popular poker game.

3. *Hold'em is the most widely played casino poker game in the world. You are just about guaranteed to find a low-limit game.* This book is about beating the low-limit game. The popularity of Hold'em means that you are almost certain to find a low-limit game in any decent-sized casino. Hold'em remains the premier live poker game in casinos worldwide. There is no casino in North America that would dream of opening a poker room without spreading Hold'em. This means that you can travel the United States, Canada, and most of the world, walk into a casino where poker is spread, and join a game.

Very few casinos spread games like Five-Card Draw, Lowball or Five-Card Stud, which you might have learned at home. If they do, these games are more likely to be populated by regulars and experts, and you can lose a lot of money in games like that. A sound knowledge of Hold'em is a universal poker passport.

4. *Hold'em attracts bad players.* You'll make most of your money from the basic blunders of bad players. The approach I'll teach you will mercilessly exploit their weaknesses and indiscipline. The harsh but inexorable law of poker is that over time the money ends up in the pockets of the good players at the expense of the bad. Bad players tend not to read books. In the short run, bad players can make outrageous plays and win some pots. Bless' em! It's what keeps 'em playing. When bad play is rewarded, its called "negative random reinforcement." This is the same mentality that keeps players at the slots. Since in Hold'em it seems that "any two cards can win," poor players see Hold'em as a game of luck. You and I know better. At a table, I like to foster that delusion of luck as much as possible. In the end it makes me more money. Well, aren't I the sneaky one?

5. *It is easier to fold in Hold'em: especially in the first two* **betting rounds**. I know what you are thinking: "I came to play, not fold!" Sorry! If you want to have fun by *winning*, rather than just playing, you are going to have to do a lot of folding. It will lessen your bankroll fluctuations and keep you out of trouble. In Hold'em you will mostly have very clear guidelines as to when to fold; *that is, you will mostly know when you are a big* underdog *in a given situation.* You will know which cards are worth a **bet** and which ones you should shun like a rabid dog before the first betting round. *After* the first betting round, it will mostly be clear when you should wave good-bye to the pot too, all with very low risk. So when you are a smelly hound of an underdog, fold!

6. *Hold'em won't tax your memory because there are no exposed cards or exchanged cards, and your position remains constant through each betting round.* In Hold'em you will always know what the best possible hand (the **nuts** in poker jargon) is for any given **board**. This is because your hand and everybody else's will be made up of the two cards in your hand and the five on the board. Unlike Seven-Card Stud, there are no exposed cards, which are then folded, in

other players' hands for you to remember. Unlike Five-Card Draw, you will not have to remember who took one card or two or three cards and then try to figure out their hand. Another plus is that unlike Seven-Card stud, the betting order remains the same for each round. If you are last to bet, this important strategic advantage is guaranteed to be yours for each **round** of betting.

7. *Pots are bigger.* You may not be in many pots, but you will win more than your fair share following my approach. Since a full Hold'em table consists of ten players, many people are tossing their chips in the pot, and because there are four rounds of betting, usually with a limit of three raises per round, pots can get pretty big. If you win two or three sizable pots per playing session, you can often go home with a tidy winning sum.

8. *Jackpots are bigger.* When a very good hand gets beaten by a better one (often against the odds), it's called a **bad beat**. In most casinos, a small sum is taken from every pot and put in a **jackpot** fund. If you get a certain kind of bad beat, you win a large part of this jackpot, and so do others at your **table**. Since Hold'em is so popular and many hands are played per hour, it's common to see jackpots of over $50,000, often a lot more. Win one of these, and it can pay for your vacation and a present for your mother-in-law: well you can afford to be generous, can't you?

9. *You will be able to watch, enjoy, and understand televised poker tournaments.* Poker is hot and growing. A few years ago the idea that poker would be TV entertainment was a notion greeted with howls of laughter and derision at a poker table. Now it is big entertainment business. These days there are televised tournaments every week, featuring professional poker players, amateurs, and celebrities. Guess what they are playing? Hold'em. Now they are mostly playing **no-limit Hold'em**, and you will play limit Hold'em. The strategies are different, but they are the same style of poker. Hold'em is the poker game of the present, and most experts predict of the near future.

10. *If you want to graduate to bigger cash games or tournaments, Hold'em is your best foundation.* If you get the poker bug, you may decide to play bigger games or tournaments. These demand an additional range of skills beyond the scope of this book. However, what you learn here will give you the best possible foundation for moving up to higher limits and playing tournaments. Also, by learning Hold'em you will simultaneously be absorbing poker theory. This will enable you to learn other styles of poker quickly if you choose to later on. Plus as you develop greater skill, you will enjoy higher profits.

11. *You will be able to play on the Internet.* Television and Internet gambling have resulted in a poker-playing explosion. Log on, and you can find hundreds of games and play live with players from all over the world. What are they mostly playing? You guessed it, Hold'em. I'll say a little about the pros and cons of Internet poker later, but it's an excellent learning tool, as you can play on most sites with "play money." This will give you a way to play many hands in a short time and learn the game for zero financial risk. It doesn't get better than that in poker!

12. *Here is the One Big Reason to play Hold'em: It's fun!* You probably don't have a desire to become a professional player. You come to the casino for fun, right? If so, surely you should be playing the poker game that is the most fun and that's Hold'em. Most Seven-Card Stud players are instant converts because fast-moving, dynamic Hold'em allows them to play many more hands per hour. Hold'em is fun to play, is easy to learn, is thrilling and intriguing, and can be played without the possibility of huge risk.

Is there a downside? Only one: you have to learn a disciplined approach to be a consistent winner, *'cause losing ain't fun, and a wild, undisciplined approach is a losing one.* I'm here to save you hours of time and stress by giving you that strategy. So read on!

CHAPTER TWO

The Low-Limit Cash Game

IN THIS CHAPTER, I will describe some broad concepts and highlight some fundamentals of low-limit poker. In chapter 3, I will describe the basics in more specific detail. In this chapter, you may find some poker terms that you are not familiar with. I will explain most as I proceed, but to explain them all would make it too clunky to read. If there is a term that confuses you, refer to the glossary (at the end of the book) where you can find the boldfaced terms that are in the text.

What Is "Low-Limit" Poker?

Low-limit (more properly "fixed-low-limit") is both a factual description of a poker game and also a subjective description of a game that exhibits certain tendencies. Let me clarify: in any form of fixed-limit poker, the amount you can bet at any one time has a previously determined, fixed limit. In Hold'em there are four rounds of betting, which I will tell you more about later. Right now you just need to know that there are four betting rounds. If you sit down at a table spreading 2–4 Hold'em, you know that the minimum amount you can bet on the first two rounds of betting is $2, and the minimum amount you can bet on the last two rounds of betting is $4. Any of the following games would objectively be described as a low-limit game: $1–$2, $2–$4, $3–$6, $4–$8, $5–$10, $6–$12, and $10–$20.

The $10–$20 game is usually considered the watershed where you will start to find the better players playing. Why? Because they believe they can make more money at the higher limits, a fallacy that we will explore together in the next few paragraphs.

Subjectively a low-limit game, sometimes derisively labeled "no-fold 'em-Hold'em," is a type of game in which players will bet and call with all manner of weak hands. Furthermore, they will cling to these hands even when it is patently obvious to better players that they have little or no chance of winning the pot in a final **showdown**. Now, you sometimes see play like this at the higher limits but it is rare. In the low-limit games it is commonplace.

Put simply, in low-limit games you will make your money by capitalizing on the fundamental errors made by the many poor players found in these games. You know, the ones that *unlike* you, have not taken the trouble to read this book!

What will these unskilled players do? They will bet when they should raise, check when they should call, and, most important for you, play on when they should clearly fold. If you play in the way I suggest, you will not play this way. Instead, you will play somewhat conservatively but solidly and straightforwardly. Surprisingly, this approach is the sort of play that will take the money in a low-limit game. Why? Because *sophisticated and fancy plays have almost no place in the typical low-limit* game.

Now that little tidbit may come as a surprise! It may shock you to learn that players who are used to playing in higher stakes games against other good players often lose money at the lower limits. The reason is that they frequently fall victim to "fancy playitis," a poker syndrome in which a better player tries to dazzle his weaker opponent by fancy plays. But *you can only make a fancy play against a* good *player*!

A **weak** player will not understand what you are trying to **represent** by your fancy play and may ironically play correctly, almost by accident. The weaker the competition, the more straightforwardly you should play, if you want to be a winner.

Weak players will make so many basic errors that straightforward, solid play will take the money more efficiently. The strategy and tactics described in this book, if learned and followed, are meant to prepare you for this type of game and will enable you to beat almost any low-limit game over time. Also, if you ever decide to move up, this knowledge will provide the foundation for building a strong mid- and high-limit game.

A Profile of a Typical Low-Limit Game

So apart from the betting limits, what sort of players populate these games? They vary a lot from tourists who rarely play to retirees who may play every day. Some will seem to know little about the game while others will have a thousand tales of the green felt. Most play for entertainment rather than just money. They like to "gamble" a bit but are rarely too aggressive. They come to "play cards," not to play good poker. They will sometimes be wild, but are more usually too **passive**. They will tend to call too often and fold too little. They will see too many *flops* and hang around too much after the Flop. They will regale you with stories of their terrible luck as they take down the odd pot themselves with outrageous hands. They will mostly believe they are much better than they are and will tell you that "Charlie thinks he's hot stuff, but we all know he's a **fish**."

They will be surprised as you turn over good hand after good hand but still rarely give you credit for holding one. They will occasionally despise your good luck as you walk away from the table a winner yet again, and when you leave, they will shake their heads and wish they were as lucky as you were. Welcome to low-limit Hold'em!

How Casino Poker Differs from Your Home Game

I was not brought up in a poker-playing household. I cannot claim I learned my poker skills at my grandpappy's knee or watching my big brother play. I have not played in college dorms or in the navy or in the regular "Thursday Night Game." I am an artificial poker creation. My poker baptism took place not in a home game but over the green baize of Atlantic City. Many of you, however, have entirely different poker origins. You *will* have played in college or with your family or with your friends, and you may even have a grandpappy or grandmamma, who taught you the rudiments of the game. The book *Real Poker Night* by Henry Stephenson describes at length the differences and transitions from the home game to the way poker is played in public card rooms. I recommend you read his book. Right now I will only summarize some key differences.

When you step into a casino for the first time, it will most likely be bewildering. When you move beyond the clang and buzz of the slots and find your way to the poker room, you may find yourself overwhelmed by the range and choice of games being offered. Of course you are looking for the Hold'em tables, but you will probably also see Seven-Card Stud and Omaha. What you won't see are home game specials like Baseball, Follow the Queen, or Roll Your Own. You won't see games with "one-eyed jacks" and "**deuces** wild," either. What you will see is a variety of limits at maybe three to four different styles of poker. How come? The reason is that these types of home games have such high elements of chance that they diminish the skillful player's chance to make intelligent plays.

Poker is essentially a contest of skill with an element of luck. It is the balance of luck and skill that makes for an interesting poker game. If poker were all skill, then we would be playing chess. Any form of poker that entirely removes chance or uncertainty also makes for a poor game. So any poker game that demands too much luck—"a lottery game"—or has an innovation that entirely removes chance in certain cases, is one where true poker skill, the balancing of chance and certainty, is inherently dull and superficial. The reason that home games are often more like lottery games is that home poker players are less likely to understand the true depth and subtlety of "grown-up poker." They try to add color to what they see as a dull game by the inclusion of crazy rules.

True poker players like to win by making correct decisions and compelling other players to make wrong ones, not by merely watching to see whether the hand they are dealt next is a lucky one or one that means winning is certain. Good poker means consistently making good decisions. If you don't want to make decisions, don't play poker! A good poker game should mostly reward good decisions. The poker games now being offered at public card rooms and casinos are the ones that have been formulated, adapted, and played over time and are accepted by the current poker community as being the ones that offer the optimum balance between luck and skill and between randomness and complexity.

Fashions change. Texas Hold'em is now the most popular poker game worldwide. It used to be Seven-Card Stud. In old Westerns, you see Five-Card Draw as the game of choice. In the 1940s, 1950s, and 1960s, Five-Card Stud was the main game, but it is hardly ever spread now. Some thought Omaha was the game of the future, but it has proved to be popular only among a minority. Learn Texas Hold'em and you are probably good for the next twenty-five years at least. Hold'em is here to stay.

You won't see any Nickel-Dime games in public card rooms. The casino makes no money by spreading them and serious poker players don't want to play games like this. Here is why: for a poker game to be enjoyable, you must value the bets you make, either as money or as markers of success. Micro-stakes mean you don't care about winning or losing, and therefore good or bad decisions make no difference. You have no respect for the game, no reason to analyze, and no chance of pain or satisfaction. How dull. You don't have to risk the farm to play serious poker, but insignificant risks mean insignificant games. No fun!

Perhaps what you will notice the most in public card rooms is the high speed of play. My first wife watched me play for the first time after I had been playing for over a year in public card rooms. Though she knew the rules and had played in one or two home games, she was overwhelmed by the game she witnessed, a very passive $3–$6 game. "It's all happening too fast for me to keep up," she complained.

I was surprised because it all felt pretty leisurely to me. I had forgotten how overwhelmed I had felt when I first entered a casino. If you feel a little intimidated at first, remember, all players feel that way when they first play. Follow the advice in this and other chapters, and you will quickly feel like a seasoned regular, yawning at the slow pace of the game.

Why Cash Games Are Better Than Tournaments for New Players

Tournaments can be tempting to the new player. Many casinos and public card rooms offer tournaments with very low entry fees. It is true that you can hang around in a tournament and have fun while you play hand after hand with that **stack** of tournament chips given to you to form your initial stake. Some casino tournaments last hours, going through many rounds. You may be lucky enough to finish in the money and take home a prize out of all proportion to your initial entry fee. More than likely, however, if you last a few rounds, you will probably bust out with only experience to show for your investment of time.

Tournaments can be lucrative, but to win, you need quite a hefty dose of luck at the right time. That means not just good cards, but good cards at just the right moment to take advantage of the instant when a large pot arises. Very few players, even top ones, are consistent tournament victors. To make a living as a tournament player, you need the right temperament, considerable skill, a fat bankroll or backers with deep pockets, and *luck*, definitely luck. Skillful tournament play and why you need luck even if you are a strong player to do well in tournaments are topics beyond the scope of this book. Here are the reasons I believe new players should develop a sound "cash game" before tackling tournament play:

• *Cash forces you to make decisions that matter.* Poker chips represent cash. You buy in for cash and check out for cash. The essence of poker is consistently making good decisions. When bad ones cost you money in the form of chips, you feel the pain. Good. If it has meaning, you will be less inclined to make a bad bet or call **loosely**. No pain, no lesson. Tournament chips by contrast feel less like real money. Let us say you bought into a tournament for $50 and got 300 tournament chips. By careful play you build it to 1,000, and in a moment of recklessness, you lose it all in a single, ill-considered confrontation in one hand.

"Well, hell, I only lost $50," you rationalize. True. Next tournament you make a similar mistake and rationalize it similarly. Learned anything? Nope. Build up $300 to $1,000 by contrast and lose *that* in a single hand of careless play, and I guarantee that you will feel pain, learn a lesson, and control yourself more carefully next time, which brings me to my next point.

- *Tournaments engender a gambling mentality.* "Just a moment—isn't poker gambling?" you ask. Not really. When you gamble against the house, you are usually playing a game you cannot win long term. When you play solid poker, you are *like* the house because you always endeavor to bet with probability *on your side*. You bet *"with the* **best of it***,"* as they say in poker circles. This does not guarantee that you will never lose a hand, a pot, or a session, but if you bet consistently with the odds in your favor, you must win over time. On such considerations and mathematics, huge casino fortunes are built. Cash games give you the best sense of this. Play well and against weaker opposition, and over time your bankroll must grow. This is positive reinforcement. In tournaments, by contrast, luck becomes a greater and greater factor as the tournament progresses, and the forced bets or **blinds** become a greater and greater percentage of your stack. In this scenario a few lucky hands and overly aggressive, reckless play can sometimes find its reward. Take that attitude to a cash game, and you are a poker disaster waiting to happen.

I love to play a cash game against people who have just busted out of a tournament. They often carry that attitude of reckless bravura into the cash game and lose chips fast. Cash games give you a sense of where you are in terms of skill; tournaments can delude you into thinking your game is better or worse than it truly is. The tournament player dreams of the big payday. The cash player is seeking to grow his wealth over time, by correct play.

- *Tournaments are time inefficient.* When I played poker to supplement my meager salary, I played in cash games. I knew that as a winning player, the more hours I played, the more I won. My bankroll grew. I put in the hours and "punched the poker clock," so to speak. Not glamorous, but effective. I knew what my hourly win rate was. Even if it came in fits and starts, I was making money. In a tournament I might play well for six hours, get busted out, and what had I earned? Zilch, zero, not a red cent. I was chasing the big payday instead of being content to book modest but consistent wins. Booking wins makes poker fun each time you play. It encourages good play and makes you more resolved to play well the next time too.

- *Tournaments are sometimes more expensive than they appear.* Many tournaments allow multiple re-buys. Some players re-buy as many times as they are allowed. If you have a tournament with a $100 *buy-in*, and you make five $60 re-buys and then bust out, you have effectively nothing to show for your $400 investment. Do this two or three times a week, and it can start to get costly. Far better is to put this into your poker bankroll, find a game at a suitable level, and start building that bankroll up.

  In conclusion, start with cash games (sometimes called **ring games**) and build your skills. I believe you will show greater profit over time and have more fun. If you want to enter a tournament, first read some of the books in this book's bibliography found in chapter 12 and only enter after you have played at least one hundred hours in cash games.

Internet Card Rooms: Should You Play Poker Online?

Some of you may have heard of a newfangled invention called "The Internet." Internet card rooms and casinos have exploded in growth in the last few years. Combined with newly televised poker tournaments, Internet poker has been primarily responsible for the enormous numbers of new players entering the game. Among the large poker sites, it is not uncommon for there to be over 10,000 people playing at one time, online, across hundreds of tables. Internet card rooms are strange, as there are no cards, at least physically, and no room! At one table you may find yourself playing in real-time with your next-door neighbor and simultaneously with players in Europe, South America, Australia, the Middle East, and, of course, all over the United States. People who have no terrestrial casinos within hundreds of miles can have more Internet poker games to choose from than residents of Las Vegas do.

It seems like the most convenient way to play, so the question is, Should *you* play poker over the Internet? Hold it! Online poker has a number of advantages but also some significant disadvantages, especially for the poker novice. What follows is a brief examination of some of the pros and cons of playing poker on the Internet. Online poker has a definite role to play in your poker education, but it is not always the card players' Shangri-La that it is made out to be.

The Advantages of Playing Online Poker

Whole books have been devoted to the merits of online poker. What follows is by no means an exhaustive discussion but only highlights of some salient points. Here are a few of the pros of Internet Poker:

1. *You can play anywhere, anytime.* If you have access to a computer and a connection to the Internet, you can play. Since there are

dozens of card rooms with hundreds of games and thousands of **active players** in multiple time zones, you can *always* find a game somewhere on the Internet.

2. *No travel times.* The casino comes to you. No traveling. No time off from work. No need to book a hotel room. You can play in your bedroom, living room, or office or anywhere you have an Internet link. You can play in your underwear or in the bath, while having a drink, listening to music, or munching a grotesque-looking sandwich. No one knows or cares. You can play for five minutes or ten hours. You can even play two or more games at once, for different stakes, and even different types of poker, if you want a real challenge.

3. *You can use supplementary information to help you make the correct decisions.* Most regular, physical casinos do not even allow reading at the table, let alone reading poker books. Even if you are allowed to refer to a "crib sheet" at the table, you will then identify to the other players that you are an inexperienced player. Online, you can have tables, charts, books, and computers all around you if you wish. No one knows or cares. Most Internet casinos even show you the exact amount in the pot, enabling you to make instant calculations.

4. *Your overheads are lower.* The **rake** (the amount the casino takes from each pot, which is how it makes its profit) is usually lower than for a physical casino. Also, you do not have to tip the dealer, another customary expense of a regular casino.

5. *You can get more playing opportunities.* Since there is no dealer and no physical movement of cards or chips, you can play many more hands per hour. This makes the game move along very quickly. If you are a winning player, this means you can win more money per hour. Online poker is great for the antisocial. You do not have to chat with, or be vexed by, the person next to you, and you are

not subject to all those bad beat (bad luck) stories that seem to be a part of almost every poker table.

6. *You can start playing for much lower stakes.* The smallest game in most terrestrial casinos is $2–$4. Online, by contrast, you can find games as low as $0.25–$.50 (twenty-five and fifty cents) and $1–$2. The very low overheads of Internet casinos make this possible. This means that you can start with a micro bankroll. You can even start with no bankroll! What? Online casinos usually allow you to try your hand at poker using a fictional bankroll or play money as it is often called. Later, in this chapter, I will show you how you can use this facility as a learning tool to improve your poker skills.

Raring to play Internet poker? Wait a minute, buddy. There are thorns as well as roses in that garden. Online poker has a number of major disadvantages too, and these are doubly so for the new player. Let me list them for you right now.

The Disadvantages of Playing Online Poker

1. *Online games are usually much tougher than the equivalent stakes games at regular casinos and card rooms.* This surprises many people and some even deny this to be true. Surely, they argue, with all those novices in the game, the games are soft. Not exactly true and here is why: players who delude themselves into believing they are winners in live games quickly discover they are in fact losing players when they play online. In a terrestrial casino, it may take players years to realize that they are cumulative losers. Poor record keeping, by which I mean not accurately recording wins and losses, means that the some players can delude themselves for a long time into believing they are much better than they are. Good players take advantage of, and may even encour-

age, this delusion, telling the weak player that his (the bad player's) luck is bound to turn around soon.

The speed and relentless nature of online play often ensures that poor players lose fast, and their lack of skill is starkly apparent. What happens to the poor players then? They quit. This means that there is a constant thinning out of poor players online, just as there is a constant flow of new ones. The cumulative effect is that on the popular sites the bad disappear and the good play on, making the games tougher. A $5–$10 game online with "regulars" playing may be tougher than a $15–$30 game in a regular casino.

2. *Online poker games can seem blindingly fast to the new player.* If you have only played poker in home games, you will be surprised at how fast the games move along in a regular casino. On the Internet this is doubly so. Furthermore, the other players will have zero tolerance for slow play. Some online casinos even allow you to vote "abusive" players off the table, and the most common abuse is slow play. While, theoretically, you have the time to calculate odds, consult charts, books, and computers when playing on the Internet, in practice you will hardly ever have time to do so. Beginners tend to find this very intimidating, and the added pressure of a rapidly dwindling bankroll can result in your making poor poker decisions.

3. *You can lose track of how much you are putting into the game.* For online poker you need to set up an account with the casino. You might be conservative and charge your credit card for $50. You get your feet wet and lose it fast. "I know the problem," you say. "My bankroll was too small. I'll buy in for some serious money."

Now you load up with $500 but still start to lose. "Can't play 'real' poker in these penny ante games," you rationalize. "I better move up a few levels, and of course I'll need a bigger bankroll." So you buy in for $2,000. Now you win a few and lose more, but so what? You can always charge a "little more" to the card to overcome your run of temporary bad luck. Besides, with minimum monthly payments, it is only costing you about $200 a month. Cheap entertainment, you muse. Within a short while, you have a running credit card debt of over $5,000 or more. Somehow poker is not as much fun as it used to be. You have become a gambler, not a poker player. In a regular casino, by contrast, you usually have to buy in with cash and check out with it. Once again it feels *real* and keeps you honest. It is much easier to keep track of your wins and losses too.

4. *The fact that you can start with such low stakes means you do not take it seriously.* If you play for sums that are so small that they have no meaning to you, you will be less likely to concentrate on making good poker decisions. Playing for $0.25 a hand is hard to take seriously. Booking a "big win" in this game for $13.75 is hardly likely to make you feel much excitement. You should never play over your head, but if wins and especially losses have no meaning for you, you will tend to play loosely and badly.

5. *Steaming can be frequent and costly online.* **Steaming**, or going on **tilt**, is when a poker player becomes emotional and starts to play wildly and badly. It usually follows a bad beat when another player beats you out of a pot by getting a stroke of extra good fortune and winning against the odds, say by **drawing** an improbable hand against you. Now you feel sorry for yourself.

   "I don't care what Myers says," you rant. "You can't beat those lucky SOBs. They don't know what good play is. I'll show them," you mutter, "I'll play just as stupidly as them. That'll teach them."

   So swearing vengeance, you start to play crazy poker until the mood passes or the chips run dry. Steaming players are found in regular casinos too. I'll tell you more about them and how to avoid being one in chapter 4. Steaming while playing on the net is more likely. Playing on your own, the fear of embarrassing yourself in public is absent. At home, you can shout, scream, kick the dog, and play like a jerk, and only you, your opponents, and your bankroll will know. You have abandoned your careful poker plans. This is a sure way to go through money fast!

6. *You get no human feedback or* **tells** *online.* When you play in a live casino, you can learn a lot by observing other players, who look worried, nervous, excited, bored, tired, or even drunk. These things all affect how your opponents play. Tells, characteristics or mannerisms that betray a player's thinking, are almost entirely absent online. In live play you have a wealth of visual and auditory information to inform your play and help you win.

7. *Playing online is lonely not social.* If you are not playing poker professionally, I maintain poker should be *fun*. What is the sense of playing and being miserable? Part of the fun is meeting new characters and enjoying nonpoker conversations. Online chat is limited. I have played poker and had stimulating conversations at the table with doctors, lawyers, farmers, horse breeders, CEOs, professional sports people, an Alaskan gold miner, a diplomat, a number of famous Broadway and movies stars, and an exotic-animal trainer, to name just a few. Playing poker on the Internet can sometimes make you feel like a video game geek.

Conclusion

So am I telling you never to play on the Internet? Not at all. I do regularly. I am saying that when you play for cash you should do so live, at first, if you can, and take my warnings about Internet play seriously. As your game improves, you can then play on the Internet. I believe you will find live games easier to beat and handle at first. That said, the Internet does have a very important role to play in your development as a poker player: *you can practice your new knowledge and skills for absolutely* no risk whatsoever *on the Internet, and I strongly encourage you to do so.*

When I learned poker, I was lucky. Good, if somewhat poorly written books were available and so was the computer. I purchased a program that enabled me to get the basics down cold by playing simulations against computerized opponents. This effectively let me experience years of play in weeks. I did not have to spend long years and big bucks learning the basics. I built the foundation of a solid game *before* I ever stepped into a casino. Now you can do much better than I did. Here is how and why: right now you can set up an account with a number of online casinos and play for free with the play money I described earlier. Unlike me, you can play against real people in real games, where you know the rules will be followed to the letter. It is the ideal way to practice when you first start to play. If you ever decide to learn a different form of poker, say Seven-Card Stud or Omaha, you can test the waters this way and see if you like it and see how you do. You can practice anywhere, anytime you wish, as long as you have access to a computer and an Internet connection.

Do this first, and you will greatly shorten your learning curve. A word of caution, though: play money games are not exactly like the real thing. Players tend to call excessively and hang on to the end. Also, they tend to be more reckless, like an exaggerated form of the typical low-limit game. If you can do well in these games, you will have established a solid foundation for live casino play in minimum time at no risk. What a deal!

CHAPTER THREE

Texas Hold'em Basics

Fixed-Limit Hold'em: The Basic Rules of Play

THE OBJECT OF Texas Hold'em, as in all poker games, is to accumulate as much money as possible. You win money by winning the pot. The pot is the sum total of all bets made during the course of a hand. There are only two ways to win a pot:

1. *Be the last player remaining:* If every other player has folded their hand, this means that they have forfeited any interest they have in that pot. The last player remaining wins the pot.

2. *Have the highest-**ranking** hand at the **showdown**:* If two or more players continue to contest the pot, then after the last playing round, there is a showdown where the players reveal what cards they hold. In this case, the player with the highest-ranking hand will win.

Every casino I know of uses the **cards speak rule**. This rule states that players do not have to state the contents of their hands correctly. The dealer will award the pot to the player showing down the best hand, regardless of any statement made by the player. Novice Hold'em players sometimes get confused as to exactly what hand they are holding. On more than one occasion I have seen a player prematurely throw

23

in a hand or "**muck** the hand" as poker players say, only to realize that he in fact had the winning hand. Don't do this. When a hand hits the muck, the pile of folded and discarded cards, it is declared dead. At the showdown, simply turn over your hand and let the dealer award the pot.

Some players throw in their hand after they see another hand out-ranks theirs at the showdown either because of disgust or embarrass-ment or because they do not want others to see their hand. If you call a player at the end, you have a right to see the hand. The rule **show one, show all** means that if one player has seen the hand, every player at the table has a right to see it. I played in a tournament once when a player on seeing his opponent's called hand tossed his own hand in the direction of the dealer in flamboyant disgust, intending to muck his cards. He quickly realized that he had acted impetuously and that in fact, his hand was the best hand. Well, his card did not actually touch the muck but had hit the dealer's hands and bounced back to him. He claimed his cards were live. His opponent claimed he had mucked the hand and forfeited the pot. A heated discussion ensued where many players exchanged passionately held but differing opin-ions as to what the correct rule was in this instance. The tournament referee was called. The cards were ruled live. Why? "The dealer is not the 'muck'," the referee stated with the air of King Solomon.

"It is nice to have official confirmation that you are in fact not muck, don't you think?" I asked the dealer.

"You would never know that the way we are treated by some play-ers around here," he retorted.

As a new player, just turn your cards over at the end, it's simpler!

The Ranking of Poker Hands

Only one deck of cards is used to play poker. The ranking of hands in poker where the highest hand wins (poker played for "high" or reg-ular poker) is always the same. If you have played poker before, you can skip this section. In a later section in this chapter, I am going to show you how these hands appear in a community card poker game, such as Hold'em where cards are shared. Poker hands are made up of five cards. They are ranked in order of the probability of them occurring. The rarer the likelihood of them being dealt, the higher their rank. In poker, rarity creates value. Here is their ranking and therefore rarity, starting with the highest and rarest and ending with the lowest and commonest:

The highest-ranking hand is a **straight flush**, that is five cards of the same **suit**, in sequential order. The highest possible straight flush is called a "royal flush." A royal flush is the best possible hand in poker.

Here is royal flush:

Here is a straight flush:

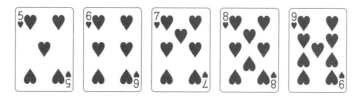

The size of any poker ranking is determined by the ranking of the highest card. In the previous example, this hand could only be beaten by a straight flush of a higher rank. For example:

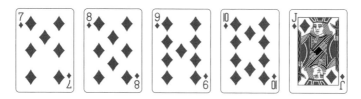

The next highest hand is four of a kind. This is four cards of the same rank. Since there are only four suits in a deck of cards, this hand is composed of four cards, one of each suit. The rank of the fifth card is irrelevant. Of course, four tens beat four nines and four jacks beat four tens. The highest four of a kind holding is four aces.

The next highest hand is a **full house**. In poker slang this is sometimes called a **boat** or "full boat." A full house consists of three cards of one rank and two of another.

Here is an example:

This hand is called *"aces* full of *jacks."*

Here is another:

This hand is called *"jacks* full of *aces."* The hand is always described by naming the three, same-ranked cards first. The first full house outranks the second, as the rank of the three-card set determines how high the full house ranks in comparison to other full houses. The rank of the second two cards determines the seniority of rank if the first three are the same, an important consideration in a community card style of poker, such as Hold'em. For example:

$$A\spadesuit, A\clubsuit, A\heartsuit, Q\spadesuit, Q\spadesuit$$

would outrank

$$A\spadesuit, A\clubsuit, A\heartsuit, J\spadesuit, J\spadesuit$$

but

$$A\spadesuit, A\clubsuit, A\heartsuit, K\spadesuit, K\spadesuit$$

outranks

$$A\spadesuit, A\clubsuit, A\heartsuit, Q\spadesuit, Q\spadesuit$$

A **flush** is the next highest hand. A flush consists of any five cards of the same suit.

Here is one:

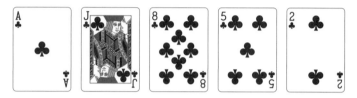

Once again the rank is determined by the rank of the highest card. An ace-high flush is the highest, followed by a king-high flush, and so on, down the ranks.

Next in order is a **straight**. A straight consists of five cards in sequential numerical order but of differing suits.

Here is an example:

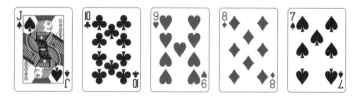

Yes, you guessed it; this is a jack-high straight. A queen-high straight would be higher and a ten-high straight, lower.

The next highest is **three of a kind**. Later in this chapter you will see that this is sometimes also called a "set." It consists of three cards of the same rank and two other cards of any rank or suit not paired.

Here is an example:

The next highest hand is called "two pair." As you would expect, it consists of two separate **pairs** of cards of differing ranks and a fifth card of any suit or rank.

An example is:

In poker circles this is called "kings and jacks." This hand:

outranks it because the highest pair, in this example the pair of aces, outranks the pair of kings. If the **top pair** of the two pair is the same, the rank of the **second pair** governs the overall rank of the hand.

outranks

The final and lowest ranking hand is a pair, a pair of cards of the same rank and three other cards of any rank or suit.

For example:

This is a pair of queens, of course. Strictly speaking, a pair is the lowest-ranking hand. However, at the showdown it can happen that no player even holds a pair. If that is the case, then the player holding the highest card (aces through twos) wins. If two players hold the same high card, the second highest card plays, and so on down.

Split Pots

Suits are not ranked in Hold'em. If one or more players hold the same five cards at the showdown, the chips in the pot are split between them.

Hold'em and Community Cards

Hold'em, unlike Five-Card Draw or Seven-Card Stud, is a form of community card poker. This means that instead of players being dealt a series of cards individually to make up their hands, each player's hand is composed of cards dealt to them plus a number of cards shared by *every* player. This shared pool of cards is known as the board and is dealt face up in the middle of the table for all players to see.

In Hold'em, each player is dealt two cards face down. These cards are called your **pocket cards**. Your hand consists of the best five cards combining your pocket cards plus the board of community cards. In Hold'em, the board is composed of five cards. You may use one, two, or none of your pocket cards to form your hand. If you use neither of your pocket cards to form your hand, it is called **playing the board**.

Now, I would like to illustrate hand rankings as they would appear in a Hold'em game, consisting of your **pocket pair** plus the five cards on the board.

A royal flush:

You hold:

The board is:

(The last two cards are irrelevant to the hand **value**.)

A straight flush:

You hold:

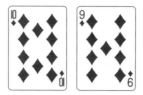

The board is:

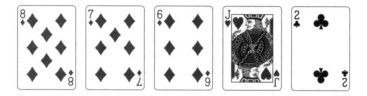

(The last two cards are irrelevant to the hand value.)

The same hand but your pocket cards are different and the board is different, and you still have a straight flush:

You hold:

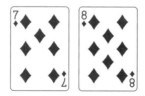

The board is:

(The last two cards are irrelevant to the hand value.)

Four of a kind:

You hold:

The board is:

(The last three cards are irrelevant to the hand value.)

A full house:

You hold:

The board is:

(The last two cards are irrelevant to the hand value.)

The same hand, but this time you do not hold a pocket pair. (You would only have played this hand as a "free" play, checking in the **Big Blind**!)

You hold:

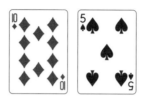

The board is:

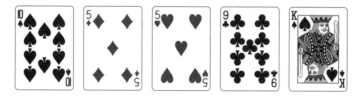

(The last two cards are irrelevant to the hand value.)

Two different configurations of a flush:

You hold:

The board is:

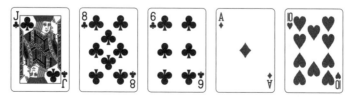

(The last two cards are irrelevant to the hand value.)

You hold:

The board is:

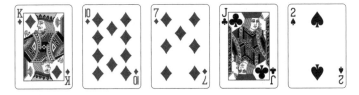

(The last two cards are irrelevant to the hand value.)

Three of kind or **trips**:

Here is a **set** of trips, or three of a kind. When you have a pocket pair, trips are called a "set."

You hold:

The board is:

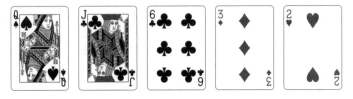

(The last four cards are irrelevant to the hand value.)

Trip queens:

You hold:

The board is:

(The last three cards are irrelevant to the hand value.)

Two pair:

You hold:

The board is:

(The last three cards are irrelevant to the hand value.)

You can also have two pair if you hold a pocket pair and another pair is on the board.

A Pair:

A pocket pair is obviously two cards of the same rank, but if you hold only one of a rank and another of the same rank appears on the board, this also makes your pair.

Here is an example:

You hold:

The board is:

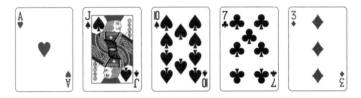

Your final hand is a pair of aces with a king as your **kicker** card. (The last three cards are irrelevant to the hand value.)

Betting Limits

In fixed-limit Hold'em (more commonly just called "limit Hold'em") each of the four betting rounds has a predetermined amount that each player can bet or raise in that round. In Hold'em there are *four betting rounds*. In fixed-limit Hold'em, the amount you can bet or raise on the last two rounds of betting is double the amount of the first two betting rounds. For example, in $2–$4 Hold'em, you can bet or raise in increments of $2 on the first two rounds and bet or raise in increments of $4 on the last two rounds.

Most casinos place a limit of three raises in each betting round. The exception to this rule is if only two players are contesting a pot (called **heads up** play), then, at that point, the casino usually allows an unlimited number of raises.

Here are some examples from a $2–$4 game: If you wish to call on the first betting round then you must put $2 in the pot. If you wish to raise on that same betting round, then you must put $4 in the pot. If there has already been a raise in that round, it will cost you $4 to call that bet and *$6 to re-raise. In poker, a betting round ends when* all *players have had an opportunity to act and* all bets, for the players that remain in the pot, are equal. *Those two events signal the end of the betting round.*

Low-limit Hold'em covers any game where the limits range from $2–$4 up to and including $10–$20. Generally, beyond this betting limit, and even sometimes at $10–$20, the games start to change in character, becoming tougher as the skills and sophistication of the players improves. You will need skills beyond the scope of this volume to do well in these games, so avoid them for now.

Poker Actions

In poker, when it is your turn to act, or as poker players say, "The action is on you," there are only five possible actions that you can take:

FOLD

You push your cards face down toward the dealer. You can also say **fold** when you do this. The dealer then puts your hand, along with any others that have been folded, into a pile of cards (the muck), all face down. These cards are out of play and so are you at least for this hand.

CALL

All bets must be equal. When poker players say, "I'll see you," it means that if you call, you will have to put an amount into the pot that is equivalent to the most recent bet or raise.

RAISE

To **raise** means to match *and increase* a bet made by a player who has acted before you. In fixed-limit poker the amount of this raise is governed by the limit of the game. In $2–$4 Hold'em, for example, bets and raises must be in increments of $2 in the first two rounds of betting and in increments of $4 in the last two rounds. So the first raise at this limit would be to $4, the second to $6 and the third (casinos usually allow only three raises) will be to $8. Always clearly announce that you are going to raise to the dealer before you move or touch your chips. In public card rooms, you are not allowed to make a **string bet**. That is going back to your pile of chips to get more in order to raise. All chips going into the pot must be put in in one motion *unless you declare a raise before touching your chips.* If you do not do this another player may call, "string bet," and you will only be allowed to call. The reason for this rule is to stop the unethical practice of putting into the pot just enough to call, seeing what the reaction of other players is, and then leaving open the possibility of raising.

RE-RAISE

If the pot has already been raised before the action gets to you, you can re-raise it. For example, in our $2–$4 game, a player before you calls and another raises. When the action gets to you, you can re-raise. Did you work out how many chips you would need to put in? If your answer is anything other than "six," reread the last paragraph. If you say "raise" after another player has raised before you, the dealer will know you mean to re-raise. When all players have had an opportunity to act and all bets are equal, the dealer will gather them into one pile (the pot) and that round of betting is then over. If the maximum number of raises allowed (three usually) is made in any one round, the pot is said to be **capped**, and if you wish to play, you may call the bets made but you can make no further raises.

CHECK

To check is an action that indicates you are not betting while retaining the option of calling or raising later in the betting round. In the first round of Hold'em you cannot check unless you are in the big blind position, which I will say more about in the next section. In this position, you must put a bet into the pot before your hand is dealt.

Since there is already a blind or forced bet in the pot, all other players in the first round only have the option to call that bet, raise it, or fold. In subsequent rounds, if the action has gotten to you and there are no bets made yet, you can call "check." Once a bet has been made, you can only call, raise, or fold.

To **check-raise** means to raise after you have initially checked and the action gets back to you. This is a tactical play, which in Hold'em has many advantages, as we shall discover in chapter 6. Check-raising, or **sandbagging** as it can be derisively called, is sometimes considered unethical and some home games ban it. This view that check-raising is somehow unethical is utter nonsense and is only held by the childish or very inexperienced poker player. It is as idiotic as saying **bluffing** is unfair or "ungentlemanly." If you ever find a casino that bans check-raising, walk right out. The check-raise is an integral part of limit Hold'em strategy and tactics. Any Hold'em game played without this option is not worth playing.

The Big Blind and the Small Blind

In most poker games there is a forced bet, or **ante**. This is a small sum, usually much less than the minimum bet, that players must put into the pot before any cards are dealt. Without the ante, the optimum strategy would be to wait for the best possible hand and only play that hand. If everybody played this way, then you would know to fold every time somebody bet and only play with the best possible holding. A pointless exercise and not much fun! The ante forces you to play, or you would "ante away" all your money waiting for the best hand.

In Hold'em there is no ante put in by each player to begin a round, but instead two forced bets are made called the "blinds," short for blind bets. The Big Blind is usually equal to one whole, first-round bet. In our $2–$4 game this would be $2. The **Small Blind** is usually half the big blind or sometimes a third. In a $3–$6 game, for example, the Small Blind is usually $1. I'll tell you precisely how these forced bets are made later in this chapter.

Table Stakes

Remember those old films in which people at the poker table take out their jewelry and the farm deeds so that they can stay in the hand and call a bet? Well it does not happen that way in a casino or any serious game because of the **table stakes rule**. This rule states that a player may not go into his pocket (or anyone else's for that matter) for extra money during the play of a hand. The total he may gamble with is the sum he has in front of him, on the table or his table stakes. If he runs out of chips during a hand and cannot continue to call bets, he does not have to borrow money from Great Aunt Freda, give up his gold wedding ring, or rush to the cash machine. Instead, a **side pot** is created in which he has no interest. His only interest is in the original or **main pot**, and the hand continues with the remaining players playing for the main pot *and* the side pot. A corollary of this rule, enforced in almost every casino, is that a player may not remove chips from the table until he is ready to leave his seat, leave the game, and cash out by turning his casino chips back into cash. By the way, in a casino you always play with chips at the table, each denominating a stated value, never with cash. You can always add more to your original stake by buying chips from the dealer at the table.

The Dealer

Unlike a home game, the dealer is not part of the game but a casino employee whose role is to deal the cards, distribute chips, regulate the game, collect bets, assemble pots, and award them to the winning player in each hand. The casino makes *its* money by taking a small amount from each pot, usually a fixed ratio, with a maximum cap called a "rake" or by charging players a fixed sum of money or "time charge" by the hour or half hour. In poker, you play against other players, *not* the house. The function of the house is to ensure that the game is honest and properly regulated and to give players a congenial environment in which they can gamble legally.

Number of Players

A full Hold'em game, with all seats filled, is played with ten players. Occasionally, there will be an eleventh player, but this is uncommon in most casinos. This number is larger than for say Seven-Card Stud, where a table is considered full with eight players playing. This does not mean that ten players must be present to start a game. Some casinos will start with as little as two players, though most will wait for at least five to take their seats before the dealer will start to deal. This is because many players are uncomfortable with **shorthanded** play, that is, less than five or six players. I will describe shorthanded play later in chapter 9. For now, I recommend that you do not play at any table with less than six players already seated. Shorthanded play demands special skills, which for now, at least, you do not have, and if you sit in a shorthanded game, you may lose money fast. For now, just do not play in them.

This will not be a problem for you, as most casinos want to have the table as full as possible so that they can use as few dealers as possible and seat as many players as their card room allows. You will frequently be playing with between seven and ten players, as some people take bathroom breaks, eat lunch, or leave the table and no new players take their places. This is fine, as the strategy and tactics in this book are meant to be used in games in which seven to eleven players are playing.

Play of a Hold'em Hand and the Sequence of Betting

After all the previous explanations, generalizations, and preamble, you are, at last, going to see how a Hold'em hand is actually played. Here we go:

THE SHUFFLE

Strictly speaking, this is not of course a betting round, but it always happens when a new hand starts. The dealer **shuffles** the deck in the middle of the table, usually "cutting" and "riffling" the deck at least threes times. On the final cut, the dealer takes the top card and **burns** it by placing it on the bottom of the deck so that the two cards are face-to-face. This is to prevent any player from seeing the bottom card in the dealer's hand and gaining an advantage. In all casino games in the United States that I have played in, the dealer holds the deck of cards in his hands to deal. In other countries, especially the United Kingdom, I have seen dealers deal from a "shoe," or cardholder, as in Blackjack.

THE PRE-FLOP: THE FIRST TWO CARDS

The nominal dealer is marked by the presence of a small disk placed in front of one of the players. This disk is known as the **button**. The button moves clockwise around the table at the conclusion of each hand. The movement of the button signifies that a new hand has begun and indicates who is the nominal dealer. If the game were self-dealt, there would be no need for a button because it would be obvious to the players who were dealing the cards. In a casino, since the dealer is a professional, house employee and always does the physical dealing, the button is used as an indicator of the theoretical dealer. Unlike Seven-Card Stud, the order of betting remains the same for each round of betting, and it only changes at the end of the hand when the button moves. This is a *very* important consideration in correct Hold'em play and I'll be talking a lot about **position** later on in this chapter.

The player immediately to the left of the dealer **posts** the Small Blind. The person two seats to the left of the dealer posts the Big Blind. When the blinds are in place, the dealer deals the cards clockwise around the table, starting to his left with the Small Blind. He deals one card to each player face down, and when he completes a circuit of the table, deals a *second* card to each player, also face down. These are known as a player's pocket cards.

The first betting round then begins, starting with the player to the left of the Big Blind. Since the Big Blind is equal to one full bet, the first player, described as the player **under the gun** in poker parlance, can only do three things: call the bet by equaling the Big Blind, raise the blind by the agreed limit, or fold his cards.

Each player is then asked in clockwise order what he wishes to do. When it is your turn to act, the **action** is said to be on you. When each player has had a turn to act and all bets are equalized, the dealer sweeps the bets into a pile in the middle of the table (the pot) and the Pre-Flop betting round is done.

THE FLOP

The dealer then takes the top card from the deck and places it face down and unseen to his left along with the other cards that have been discarded by the players. This pile is called the "muck." This card is described as burned, and a card is similarly burned at the start of each betting round.

The dealer then places three cards face up in the middle of the table. This is the Flop. Moving clockwise and starting with the player immediately to the left of the button, the dealer asks each player what they wish to do. The player can check or bet, if there has been no bet, or fold, call, or raise, if there has been a bet. When the bets are equalized, the dealer adds the chips to the pot and the round is over.

THE TURN

The dealer burns another card and then places *one* card to the (his) right of the last Flop card face up. Another betting round begins, starting with any players remaining, to the left of the button. When all bets are equal, the round of betting is over.

THE RIVER

The final community, or board card, is called the **River**. Another card is burned and the dealer deals the River card and places it face up to the right of the Turn card. The whole board of community cards is now exposed. There is another final round of betting. Once the bets are equalized, and if more than one player is contesting the pot, there is a showdown when the remaining players expose their initial two pocket cards. The player whose bet was last called must showdown first, and then followed by the other players, from the called players left, proceeding clockwise. The dealer then awards the pot to the best hand composed of the two pocket cards plus the board of community cards. The dealer then moves the button one place to the left, the two blinds are posted, the cards are shuffled, and a new hand begins.

There you have it. Once you get past the poker jargon, it is all quite simple.

Position: What It Means and Why It Is Important in Hold'em

Position in Hold'em refers to where you are in relation to the dealer button. Position is one of the most important and least understood concepts among new players. Simply stated, being on the button is the best position because, with the exception of the first betting round (the Big Blind is the last to act in the first betting round), you will be last to act in every betting round. This gives you the enormous advantage of knowing what each player has done before you act. It confers such a huge advantage that the button moves around the players so that every player gets a turn at being on the button and having the advantage of position. Later on, you will see how position determines whether you will even play certain hands and, if so, how.

Most novice players understand that high cards are better than low and suited better than nonsuited. Most fail to understand how position affects the strength of their hands, and therefore they play hands they should fold and incorrectly play hands they should play because they have not considered positional factors. This will probably be as clear as mud to you right now, so let me give you two examples: you have a pair of aces before the Flop and you are on the button. You have the strongest hand possible, Pre-Flop, and you are in the best position. If another player bets or raises before the action gets to you, you will raise or re-raise. You will have acted correctly and maximized the amount of money you can get into the pot for that round. Your position allows you to play your strong hand flawlessly.

Take the same hand under the gun, and it becomes more difficult to build a pot and maximize your advantage. With this powerhouse hand, it is always good poker to raise and re-raise pocket aces from any position. However, let's say you raise under the gun. Every other player might fold or some might fold who would otherwise have called if you had merely called the "blind bet." You have driven other players out of the pot and thus lessened your action. Of course, it is still the correct play to raise, but your position means that you cannot maximize the amount of money that goes into the pot when you have a high probability of winning the hand, and at this point, you certainly have the best cards.

Another example: you are first to act before the Flop and you have a pair of threes. This is a hand that you will later discover you should rarely, if ever, play from this position. Here is why: suppose you call, hoping to get another three on the Flop and therefore have a set of well-disguised trip threes. If players acting after you have strong hands, they will probably raise or re-raise. You will now have to fold your hand because if you call the raises, you know that the odds are strongly against you, and your opponents almost certainly have you beaten. You have wasted a bet, or, worse, you will make a costly error by loosely calling a raise or two raises. Now take the same hand, but this time you are the last to act. Seven players have called bets ahead of you, indicating that probably none has a very strong hand. Now you have the odds to call a bet. (Note: even if one of the blinds raises, if most of the other players call, you still have favorable odds for your play.) If you Flop a set of threes, all the other players will have to act before you, you have a well-disguised hand, and you can confidently decide to bet or raise, depending on the action before you, to maximize your advantage. If you do not Flop a set, you can easily fold the hand if there is a bet before you. You have lost a small amount, but you had a higher probability of winning a larger sum, a favorable poker scenario.

So a hand that was not playable in **early position** may become one that is very profitable, when conditions are right, from **late position**. Position has changed the way you played these cards.

EARLY, MIDDLE, AND LATE

I have already used these terms, so let me define them more clearly: in this book (referring to a standard, full, ten-player table) early position refers to the first five seats after the button, middle position refers to the next three seats after that, and late position refers to the next two seats, that is the one before the button and the button, who is last to act.

POSITION IN RELATION TO OTHER PLAYERS

Your position changes with every new hand dealt. However, your position in relation to other players remains fixed, as long as you keep the same seats. For example, you will always act after a player on your immediate right, except when that player is on the button. You will always act before a player on your immediate left, except when you are on the button. The player who acts after you is said to have position on you. *You* have position on players you act after. If a player is on your immediate right, you will have position on him in every betting round but one. If a player is sitting in a seat directly opposite yours, you will have position on that player half the time and vice versa. This aspect of position is sometimes called your "relative position."

POSITION AND SEAT SELECTION

Where you sit in relation to certain players has an effect on your game and especially your bankroll fluctuations. When you join a game at a full table, you will only have the option to sit in the first available seat. However, as players leave, any person at the table may request a seat change. The players at the table always have priority over new players joining the game as to choice of seats. I always request a **seat change** marker as soon as I sit down. This is a plastic disk given to a player by the dealer to indicate that when a seat becomes vacant, you have the first choice to take that seat or stay where you are.

So why do I do this? Well, it has nothing to do with finding a "lucky seat." Some players believe that some seats in a game are "hot" and are getting dealt good cards, while others are "cold" because the players at those seats are dealt poor cards. This, of course, is imbecilic nonsense, as every player has as good a chance of getting dealt a strong hand as every other player on each new deal, as the shuffles are random and the cards have no memory; but I should like to have ten bucks for every player who has gravely indicated to me that such-and-such a seat is hot or cold. Delusional, but common.

No, the reason is this: when I sit down, I immediately begin to assess how my opponents are playing. (In chapter 10, I will say more about different playing styles, how to spot them, and what to do with them.) I want to be to the left of players who are playing aggressively and raising a lot. That way I can see the raises coming and fold my marginal hands, which I will often have to fold on later betting rounds. This helps prevent large fluctuations in my bankroll caused by calling the raises of overly aggressive players with marginal hands. Conversely, I want passive, loose players who mostly call and call too much to my left. Since their actions are more predictable, I'll have an easier time making the right play against them, even though they are acting after me.

I don't expect you to understand all of this yet. When you have read the rest of the book, reread this section. When you have played a bit, read it again. It may seem, at first, that I am making a lot of noise about a little thing, but I'm not. Sitting on the right of a wild and aggressive player can be a miserable experience for a novice, causing confusion and high bankroll swings, as you constantly get raised and re-raised. Seat selection for me has often meant the difference between a profitable session and a losing one. As you get better you learn how to handle all types of players, but even for experts, a wild or very aggressive player can cause short-term problems, so bear in mind what I have just said.

Reading the Board: Know the Nuts

All good Hold'em players instantly know the nuts for any board. Don't get offended by my language; the nuts is a poker term and a vital one. You must learn to recognize these hands immediately. So what are they? The nuts is the best possible hand given the current board. Here is an example:

The board is:

A♣, J♣, 5♦

If you had a pair of aces, you would hold the nuts at this point because the best possible hand is three aces. If the Turn card is another club, then three aces is no longer the nuts. The nuts would now be the flush containing the king of clubs. If a jack appeared on the River, the nuts would be four jacks. So as you can see the nuts changes, but at the River, only one hand can be the nuts. Learn to recognize it instantly.

Odds and Ends: Odds, Pot Odds, and Implied Odds

Poker is a game of odds. Beyond that, it is a game of probability and positive and negative expectations. If you want to be a winning player, then theoretically, at least, it is easy. Only enter the pot with hands that have a positive expectation and only play in situations in which there is a high probability of winning. Of course, this ideal is not always possible, but it should be our constant aim. I will be speaking of odds, probability, and positive and negative expectation constantly, so a few definitions are in order.

PROBABILITY AND ODDS

Probability is the likelihood of an event occurring. It can predict the likelihood of an event happening when applied to a class or group. It is a predictor of the occurrence of events within a defined group. It can never know if that event will occur in that specific, individual instance. Probability is normally expressed as a number between zero and one. An event that has a probability of 0.6 has a 60 percent chance of happening.

In games involving chance, probability is normally expressed as odds. The odds of an event happening are expressed as two numbers separated by a colon. For example, I could say that I am a 5:2 favorite to remember my wife's birthday. That means, in seven years I will remember it fives times and forget it twice. If I survived the two years that I forgot, we would say that if you placed money on my memory over a twenty-one-year period, you would win your bet fifteen times and lose six times. If you bet the same amount each time, say $5 on my remembering and your friend bets $5 on my forgetting, you would be ahead over that twenty-one-year period, because I remembered more than I forgot, and the even sums do not reflect the unevenness of the occurrences.

If you bet on my remembering, you will win money over time, and I may possibly be alive to help you enjoy your winnings, if my wife had not killed me for forgetting those six times in twenty-one years.

Your bet would have a positive expectation over the long run, but you could never predict (and neither could my wife) the years I would forget and the years I would remember. Now if on this 5:2 bet, one person was to bet $5 on me *forgetting* and another $2 on me *remembering* over the course of twenty-one years, these two people would be even. My wife would remain unhappy, but it would be a fair bet. The betting amount must reflect the correct ratios for it to be a fair bet. However, if one person bets $5 on my forgetting and the other bets $3 on my remembering, then over twenty-one years, the person betting on me remembering would come out ahead. How? He will have won $3 fifteen times for a win of $45 and lost $5 six times for a loss of $30. He will have a net win of $15, because his wager was unfair to the other party. The person betting against him bet too much. It is these types of situations that we exploit in poker.

Casinos make their profits on the long run of essentially unfair wagers. They give you the chance as an individual, for a short-term win, against the odds, in exchange for a long-term profit against the mass of people passing money across the tables. In poker, you make your money by playing in such a way as to manipulate your opponent into making bets against you when the odds are in your favor and you betting against him when the odds favor you.

POT ODDS

Pot odds are the odds being offered by the pot compared to the amount of money you must put into it. Suppose there is $15 in the pot at the River, when all the cards are out and your opponent bets $3. There is now $18 in the pot. To call you must put in an additional $3, and therefore you are getting pot odds of 6:1 If you have better odds than 6:1, you call, if not, fold. Regardless of the outcome of that individual hand, if you keep betting with the odds in your favor, or bet with the best of it in gambling parlance, you must win over the long term. Every time you bet against the odds, you make a mistake and lose long term.

The pot odds tell you if a draw is worth making. Imagine that a draw has a 9:1 chance of occurring. In other words, as an underdog you will make it one time in every ten bets. If you make a $3 call, there has to be at least $27 in the pot to make a $3 call correctly. If there is less, the call now has a negative expectation. Over time if you make that call repeatedly against the odds, you will lose money. If there is more than $27, your profit increases.

IMPLIED POT ODDS

Poker has a further consideration, however. When you compute odds you are asking the questions: "How much is in the pot?" and "What are the odds of my hand being the best?" or "What are the odds of me completing my draw?" When considering implied pot odds, or **implied odds** as they are usually known, you are asking a further question: "If I complete my draw, how much more money will I win than that which is already in the pot?"

How can you predict what an opponent will do? You cannot, but you can make a good guess based on observation and knowledge of his play. For example, let us say you are in a $6–$12 game. Suppose you are drawing to the ace-high flush with only one more card to come, and you suspect your opponent has two pair. Also, you are a 4:1 underdog to make the flush on the River. If the pot contains $32 and your opponent bets $12, there is now $44 in the pot. Not enough to make the call correctly, as the pot is only laying about 3.7:1. However, if you believe that if you make your draw, your opponent will call another $12 at the end, then you can act as if the pot *already contained that additional $12* and that the pot is laying odds of 56:12—in effect *better than 4:1*. Now the call becomes correct, *assuming you are sure that your opponent will call your $12 at the end*. Of course, you must also be sure you win the pot if you make your draw. If the board makes you a flush but by pairing makes your opponent with two pair a full house, you need even better implied odds to make this call correctly.

Money in the Pot Belongs to the Pot

Regardless of how much money you put in the pot, once it is there it is *no longer yours*. How it got there is irrelevant. The question is, Is the pot currently laying me correct odds or implied odds?

Why You Do Not Have to Be Constantly Figuring Odds to Play Good Poker

Poker players do not constantly figure odds on the fly. The game moves too fast to make this practical. Instead, they know the odds for the most common situations, since these occur repeatedly. Here is a list of some key Hold'em odds you should know:

The odds of being dealt any specific pocket pair: 220:1 against

The odds of being dealt a pair: 16:1 against

The odds of being dealt two **suited** cards: 3.3:1 against

The odds of flopping trips if you hold a pocket pair Pre-Flop: 7.5:1 against

The odds of flopping an ace or a king if you hold AK Pre-Flop: 2.1:1 against

The odds of a single ace flopping if you hold KK: 4:1 in favor of the KK

The odds of getting two more suited cards on the Flop if you hold two suited cards Pre-Flop: 7.5:1 against.

Here are two crucial sets of odds for play on the Flop:

If you Flop four to a flush, you are a 4.2:1 underdog to make your flush on the Turn and a 4.1:1 underdog to make it on the River, if you fail to make it on the Turn. This also means that if you Flop a four to a flush, you are a 1.9:1 underdog to make your flush by the River.

If you Flop an open-ended (either the low or high card makes the straight) straight draw you have about a 4.91:1 chance against to make the draw on the Turn or the River, and this means you are a 2.2:1 underdog to make the straight by the River if you have an open-ended straight draw.

If you have an inside straight draw, you are only an 11:1 underdog to make your straight on the next card.

Finally, if you are fortunate enough to Flop an open-ended straight-flush draw, you are a 1.2:1 **favorite** to make a straight or better by the River.

How to Compute Odds for Draws

What I have given you are the odds for the most commonly occurring Hold'em scenarios. However, there are many more and computing them is straightforward. You contrast the number of cards that make your hand (the **outs**) to the number that do not. For example, an **open-ended straight draw** on the Flop has eight outs. On the Flop, 47 cards are unseen; 8 make your hand, and 39 do not. You are 39:8, about a 5:1 underdog to make your straight on the Turn.

PART TWO

How to Play Winning Hold'em from Deal to Showdown

CHAPTER FOUR

Key Concepts

Winning by Folding: Avoiding Trouble Right from the Start

THE IDEA OF winning by folding can prove troublesome to new players, but is nevertheless a vital idea. You should view poker as a constant attempt to put yourself in situations in which there is a high probability of winning. In poker, one is rarely certain that one is in a commanding position and very rarely is one in an unbeatable position. Ironically, when you are, you may find yourself in a position so clearly superior that no other player will bet against you. You will win but a small pot. Your biggest wins will often come from hands in which you have a small but definite edge and from play in which the statistical fortune of your opponents will rise and fall without them being aware of it. Put another way, your opponents did not recognize, or refused to acknowledge, they were no longer statistical favorites to win the hand and continued to play when they should have folded. The capacity to make intelligent folds is one mark of the expert player.

The method I suggest is based on playing good, solid cards. The most important lesson you can learn is *knowing when to fold*. New poker players are often amazed at the frequency with which expert players fold. Expert players are able to play marginal hands and make profits from marginal situations. As a beginner, you will be far better off in avoiding marginal situations altogether, and the strategy that follows will show you how. While the expert can wring chips out of poor cards, he also exposes himself to greater risks and bankroll fluctuations. By following my recommendations, you will find yourself playing less than a third of the number of hands of your average opponent. When you do play a hand, you will play forcefully. Playing this way, you will not be dribbling away chips in weak situations. You will enter a hand when you play it boldly because you know you are a favorite, and you will continue to play strongly as long as you have good reason to believe that you remain so.

In a low-limit game, your opponents will still give you plenty of action because they will mostly assume that you play like them and will not credit you with the strong holding you have. You will not participate in many pots, but you will win the majority of the ones you contest. You will resolutely refuse to participate in low-probability situations but look on as other players do so. In this way you will *win by folding*.

Becoming a "Solid" Player

When I began playing poker, I remember one unusual professional. He had been a homeless person living on the streets. He got a job sweeping up at a poker club for a few dollars a night. He got hold of second-hand poker books and read them voraciously. He scraped together a small bankroll and by disciplined, intelligent play built a bankroll of a few thousand dollars. He became a full-time professional making his money in the low- and medium-limit games, mostly in Atlantic City. I paid a lot of attention to what he said about poker because he was truly making his living from it. He had no other source of income and could not afford to cherish poker fantasies as some players might. He told me that to win consistently I would have to become a solid player. I remember saying to him, "But I play tight!" meaning cautiously and selectively.

"Not tight, *solid*," he admonished.

When I watched him play, I realized what he meant. He played selectively, but when he entered a pot, he was fearsome and aggressive.

He dominated the play and pressed his advantage. He used all the tools of clever poker, including check-raising and re-raising where appropriate. He was selectively aggressive and hard to **read**. Playing a hand against him was always uncomfortable. Just when you thought you knew what he had, he acted in such a way that you doubted your analysis and played wrongly, usually too passively. I never liked being in a pot against him. This is the type of dangerous, fox-like player you ideally want to be. You, of course, won't be like this at first, but when you see a player like this, you will recognize a good player and you will seek to emulate him. He is not merely aggressive, but selectively so; not merely cautious, but patient; not simply predictable, but deceptive. This is your goal.

Losing Your Cool and How to Avoid It

Steaming or going on tilt is how poker players describe losing your cool and playing recklessly. How does it happen? You come to the card room to have a good time, determined to play well.

"I'll play like the book says," you promise yourself. "I'll wait for strong cards in good situations and maintain *discipline*," you vow. "In this way I shall propitiate the gods of poker. My good play will be rewarded by a profitable session."

Ah, hapless mortal plaything of the poker gods! You wait for a good hand, shunning trash. It arrives—a pair of kings. You boldly raise in mid-position and are called by four players.

"Fools," you muse, "how dare they challenge my kingly brothers. The Flop comes down, and, praise the gods, there is no card higher than kings.

9♣, 10♣, 2♥

The blessing of an **overpair**. You correctly bet, and two players fold but two players call. The Turn brings a jack of diamonds. You bet again and are raised! You realize what has happened. This player has a jack and he thinks he has the top pair. You determine to teach him a lesson and re-raise. He calls. The River brings a four of clubs. You are almost counting the pot. You bet out; the "foolish raiser" calls and the third player, who you almost forgot about in your excitement, raises!

"Not on a flush draw," you think. "They didn't have the odds." Confident in the power of your pocket monarchs, you raise and both players call. You proudly turn over your kings, barely able to suppress a smirk. The player who raised on the Turn barely notices you, and you know something is wrong. He looks at the player who raised on the River. That player turns over a five and six of clubs. The other player nods, flashes his nine and ten of diamonds, and mucks his hand. You just realize you came in third.

Our phantom flusher rakes in a nice pot, and you mumble, "How could you call the raises?"

"Oh, they were suited," comes the cheery reply. "Besides I *always* play 5, 6, they are my lottery numbers."

"Ignored odds, ignored cards, ignored position, and he beats me. Where is poker justice ?" you silently rage, "Myers has it wrong; it's mostly luck. Well, I'll show them," you resolve. "I'll play bad cards too; let's see how they like that!"

Your careful plan goes to rack and ruin, and you start to play any old garbage hand. You are steaming. You are on tilt.

Reading this, you may think what I describe is fanciful and could never happen to you. Imagine a similar scenario replayed five or more times during a night, and Job himself may go on tilt. Guess what? You will see players make outrageous draws in every session and you will see players call with terrible hands who will take down pots they had no business being in. If you are trying to play solid poker it may drive you nuts, but this is the world of low-limit Hold'em.

Now, of course, playing against the odds loses in the end. That is the inexorable law of mathematics. But you are playing with probability; probability always deals with a class of events, never individual events. A pair of aces is the strongest starting hand, and it will win most of the time against any other holding. If you had aces all the time and other players forgot that you *always* held aces, you would win enormous sums, but you would *not* win every pot. Probability cannot predict individual events, it only addresses occurrences of a "class," the class here being the possible two-card holdings before the Flop in Hold'em poker. That is why I would never bet my life on a pair of aces. Mathematically and statistically this is a correct poker play, but I will lose the wager sometimes: if I bet my life on it and lose, then I will not have had a very happy evening, however correct my poker.

Many of us are uncomfortable with thinking in terms of probability. We are mostly brought up to think in terms of certainty: if I jump in the air I will land; if I behave well I will get a cookie; if I am diligent I will get a raise; and if I behave correctly I will get my just and natural reward. Sorry, poker is not like this because correct poker strategy deals with probabilities. That means that you can play a poker hand correctly and still lose the pot. The player with the long shot can take down one pot or many, not enough to be profitable over time but enough to make your blood pressure rise if he keeps doing it against *you.*

Poker discipline is essential to winning play. It comes from accepting the nature of probability, understanding that odds are odds and not certainty, and realizing that you can only act to the best of your current knowledge, which in poker is always imperfect because you cannot see your opponents' hands.

In poker you can only control your own actions. The fact that you can choose to wager only in favorable situations, when you recognize them, is what separates poker from most casino games: your decisions make a difference; you can choose to bet with the best of it. This is how the house makes money at roulette, for example. No decision you make can change the essential odds of roulette that are *always* in favor of the house. To make money, the house just has to let players continue to place bets, and however well those players might do in the short run, over time the house will run them dry. On such considerations, great fortunes are built (or bilked) by the casinos.

Making Money from Players' Mistakes

Anytime you make a play in poker with positive expectations, you make money in the long run, irrespective of the individual result and vice versa. This law of poker cannot be defeated.

As a player, the only thing you should concern yourself with is making the right play, not the individual result. You can only control your decisions, not the outcome. All players make mistakes. Experts make fewer and less obvious and costly ones. *In a low-limit game you make money because most players are making fundamental errors time and time again.*

Your play (mine too) will be far from error free. It will just seem so compared to your competition. This happens at every level: if I play against the best nine players in the world, they will take my money over time because their more skillful play will compound the effect of my errors. Poker is at last a game of skill. Over time money will move from the less skilled to the more skilled.

You may find yourself nodding sagely at these pearls of wisdom, but you will feel it emotionally when someone next puts a bad beat on you and draws against the odds to beat you. Recognize that you cannot play good poker when you are emotionally out of kilter, so when the bad beats happen, as they surely must, remember what I have said. If you have to leave the table for a few minutes, take a walk, eat a hot dog, have a soothing herbal tea, but do not play when you are angry, vengeful, or emotionally irrational. You have enough to think about at the table without having to deal with your own high emotions.

Your aim should be to play the best poker you can, in a game suitable to your level and bankroll, and let the chips fall where they may. The ultimate poker gods are the laws of probability. Eventually, they are omnipotent, but sometimes it seems that their wheels grind exceeding slow. Propitiate these gods by always endeavoring to play with the best of it and playing the best poker you can. Study, observation, and thought will enable that "best" to get better and better and enable you to beat tougher and tougher games. Your poker pride should come from knowing that regardless of the outcomes, you continued to play your A-game and not fall victim to sloppy play. Do that and never steam, and you will be a poker force to be feared.

Bluffing: Why You Should Hardly Ever Bluff in a Low-Limit Game

And now, for something completely different. Well, not *that* different as you will see. Most non–poker players and new players are entranced by bluffing. Bluffing many think *is* poker after all. Yes and no. Now, I must confess I especially like winning on a bluff. Correct bluffing can greatly increase your win rate and make you difficult to play against. According to game theory (too complex for this book, but very important nonetheless), there is an exact mathematically determined regularity for optimum bluffing that will maximize the effectiveness of your bluffing. Do not get carried away with this line of thinking in trying to beat the low-limit game. In tougher games, against strong players, bluffing correctly is vital to winning play.

In low-limit games it is far less important. Here is why: the first rule of bluffing is that you cannot bluff a poor player, only a good one. Why? A bluff depends on the player you are attempting to bluff believing that you are holding cards other than the ones you in fact hold. This presupposes that he is actually *thinking* about your hand and trying to work out what you hold from your actions of calling, checking, and raising. In low-limit games, many players will hardly give any mental time to what cards you have, and when they do, it will often be superficial. Good players will analyze your hand, have confidence in their judgment, and fold if they think that is the correct play. In other words they can be bluffed. Poor players will often call out of curiosity, and this will mean that they are inadvertently making the correct play against your bluff.

Bluffing and "Implicit Collusion"

In his excellent poker text *"Winning Low Limit Hold'em,"* Lee Jones (with acknowledgment to Roy Hashimoto) coined the term "implicit collusion" to describe a phenomenon almost exclusive to low-limit poker. Collusion is an illegal activity when two or more players secretly work together to manipulate play. This is *not* what we are talking about. However, the effects of implicit collusion can make it appear that is what is happening. How so? In higher-limit games, most pots are contested between one, two, or three players. In this type of game bluffing is very important. In a typical low-limit Hold'em game, there are often six or more players contesting a pot. While you can often successfully bluff one or two players and get them to fold, it is very hard to bluff six, seven, or eight players. At least one of them is going to call you to "keep you honest"; they are effectively colluding (though unintentionally) against you and your bluff. Therefore, the chances of your bluff working against four, five, or more players is extremely small. Since there are often this many calling even at the River, bluffing becomes a low probability play in this type of game. Bluffs have to succeed frequently enough to pay for the times they fail. Since you get lots of callers in low-limit games, they are often poor plays. *You should rarely bluff in low-limit games. You will usually have to showdown the best hand to win the pot.*

Players will be bluffing a lot in the typical low-limit game. You should not join their ranks. So when can you bluff? If the pot has gotten large and is being contested by less than three players, you can occasionally, and I stress occasionally, venture a bluff. This mixes up your play nicely and may well succeed. Just don't become a "bluffaholic" in your low-limit games, as it will cost you too much money and encourage players to play against you more strongly because you will be characterized as a bluffer.

CHAPTER FIVE

Pre-Flop Play

IN HOLD'EM THERE are two key junctures in any hand: before the Flop and on the Flop. To play Hold'em well, you must thoroughly know which two cards you can play, in any given situation, before the Flop. This chapter is devoted to the subject of starting hands. Simply put, the biggest chip drainer and source of errors among poor Hold'em players is playing too many starting hands and playing them out of position. As I have already said, Hold'em is a highly positional poker game, as your position remains the same for each betting round. The aim of correctly playing before the Flop is to have a built-in advantage over your opponents. This means that you will generally be playing high cards, as these tend to do best in Hold'em. Of course, the only way to have the ultimate advantage before the Flop is to play only a pair of aces, the top starting hand.

Since your odds of being dealt aces (or any pair) are only 220 to 1, this would make for a rather dull game. You would also lose money for two reasons: First the amount you give up in blinds would outstrip your wins, and you would get no action as players would fold as soon as you began to play because everyone would know you only play aces. Even if you extended this playing philosophy to only playing the top five hands, you would still be playing too tight (selectively) to have any chance of walking away with a decent profit. Second, no hand has an unbeatable advantage before the Flop, as you need three more cards to complete a hand. So you must play hands that put you in a strong position, and then look at the Flop to determine if and how you will continue to play that hand.

It is impossible to separate the selection of starting hands from the consideration of your position. Hands that are playable in late position should be mucked in early position. As a general rule, the later your position, the weaker the starting hand you can play. Put another way, you can play more hands in late position than in early position. Don't get carried away with this though; you still need to be very selective.

One mark of the expert player is the ability to play more hands from a variety of positions. The expert player can "start behind," so to speak, and outplay his opponents as the hand progresses. You are not an expert yet. In low-limit games especially, most players overrate their skills and play too many hands. They also fail to understand how important position is and so find themselves having to make complex poker decisions beyond their level of skill. When I play at the lower limits, I play very straightforward poker. This is the way to take the money. You will get plenty of action because you will rarely get credit for your hands. Your opponents will not believe you or they are looking for the lucky **outdraw**, which they will occasionally get, but playing this way will lose them money over time.

Since you are a novice, I am going to severely restrict the number of two-card starting hands you can play. Yes, you will not be in as many pots as other players, but you will win more of the pots you are in, and your bankroll will have lower fluctuations. This will mean that you can sit down at a table with a moderate starting stake, knowing that you have little danger of busting out. You will have more fun playing this way, as you will be more relaxed, confident, and worry free. Remember, play in the way I suggest and you will have fun *and* make money. I shall now list starting hands by position. However, I am going to make two exceptions: pocket aces (a pair of aces) and pocket kings (a pair of kings).

When you curl up the ends of your cards and see these poker **monsters**, say a silent thank you to the poker gods. They are hugely dominant and powerful hands against all other two-card holdings. They will often win without improvement. When you see them you should raise, and if you can, re-raise from *any* position. Do not be afraid that you will scare away callers; you will still get them. These hands do best in pots with only one to three players, but they are so powerful that they even do well in multiway pots. Be bold and fearless when you hold them, and get as much money in the pot as you can, as early in the hand as you can. Other players are at a huge disadvantage against you. Every so often, unknown to you, your pocket kings will be up against a pair of aces. So be it. You should still bet strongly, as most of the time you will be up against inferior hands, not aces. Position is irrelevant when you have such a strong hand. When you get 'em, bet 'em hard.

I will now work from early position to last position, or "on the button" as Hold'em players say. Any hand that is playable in early position is playable in middle and late position. So it only becomes a question of which additional hands you can play as your position improves. I will give a brief explanation as to hand selection as we proceed, and you will also see how these hand selections relate to the strategy and tactics of play on the Flop, which is the subject of chapter 6.

It is important to understand which Flops are favorable to your hand. When you play any starting hand for either a call or raise or re-raise, you should have a clear idea in your mind as to what you are trying to achieve by your actions and what hand you are aiming to finish with. Every action in poker is taken for a reason. A good poker player can always give you a precise explanation for any action he takes: for example, before the Flop you sometimes raise to thin the field, at other times to build a pot; it depends on what type of hand you have, what your position is, and what action has gone before you. Poker actions can be paradoxical: sometimes for example, the best decision may be to fold, the *second* best may be to raise, and the worst decision may be to call. If it is bad to call, how can it be better to raise and best to fold, you ask? Future chapters will elucidate these concepts. Remember, the aim of every action is to maximize your chances of winning the pot or getting away from a hand and a situation that is or has become a low-probability proposition.

Hands You Can Play from Early Position: The First Three Seats After the Big Blind

Here is how you should play these hands from this position: Always raise or re-raise with these hands:

AA, KK, QQ, JJ, AK (suited), AK

Raise with these hands about one third of the time. Call with these hands the rest of the time or if a player acting before you has raised:

10 10, AQ (suited), AJ (suited), AQ, AJ, A10 (suited), KQ (suited)

Fold everything else.

In this position you are playing very tightly. With the big pairs, you aim to enter the pot strongly to dominate and to get as much money in the pot as possible. The calling hands I list are still strong hands. In a loose game you may well have the best hand, but you want to see how you stand on the Flop, and you do not want to raise too much, as hands ahead may be stronger. You add deception to your game by raising one third of the time with these hands.

Hands You Can Play from Middle Position: Seats Four, Five, and Six to the Left of the Big Blind

Raise or re-raise with any of the hands you would have raised with in early position.

If there has been a raise ahead of you, you can call with any hand you would have raised with in early position.

If there are no raisers, raise with these hands:

10 10, AQ (suited), AJ (suited), AQ, KQ (suited), KQ

If there have been two raises, raise with AA or KK, and fold with everything else.

If there are no raisers, you can call, but not raise, with:

99, AJ, A10 (suited), KJ (suited), KT (suited), QJ (suited), Q10 (suited)

Fold everything else.

The aim of raising with hands such as AQ (suited) and KQ (suited) from this position is two-fold: either you will thin the field, which is good as these hands do better against fewer players, or you will in fact have the best starting hand when others call so that getting money in the pot from players with weaker starting hands works to your advantage too.

You call with the weaker hands because these mostly do better against multiple callers. These hands are not strong enough to raise, and you need a good Flop with these hands to make them playable.

Again, you are still playing tightly and very selectively. You will be mucking far more hands than most other players at the table will. You need to be patient and selective here.

Hands You Can Play from Late Position: On the Button and Immediately to the Right of the Button

If there has been a raise and one or more re-raises, raise again with:

AA, KK

Fold the rest.

Use the information gained by being in late position. If there has been so much action before it gets to you, do not put yourself in a vulnerable position by entering the pot with hands that will almost certainly be second best. "Almost good" hands are poker's biggest chip bleeders!

If there has been one raise, *re-raise* with:

AA, KK, QQ, JJ, AK (suited) , AK, AQ (suited)

If there has been one raise, call with:

10 10, KQ (suited), KQ, KJ (suited)

If there have been *no* raises, raise with:

AA, KK, QQ, JJ, 10 10, AK (suited), AK, AQ (suited), AQ, AJ
    (suited), AJ, AT (suited), KQ (suited), KQ, KJ (suited)

If there has been no raise, call with:

99, 88, 77, A10, A9 (suited), KJ, K10 (suited), K10, QJ (suited),
    QJ, Q10 (suited),

J10 (suited), J10, J9 (suited)

Fold everything else.

As you can see, many more hands become playable from late position. Even so, I have restricted you to premium hands, unless there
have been many callers. With the hands between 99 to J9, you often
have very good odds, so a call in late position is worth it, but you still
need a lot of help from the Flop. Your hand is vulnerable to many
hands, so best to enter the hand cheaply and see what the Flop brings.
Big pairs do well in any position, but *suited connectors are great in late
position if you can enter the pot cheaply.* If you Flop a straight or flush or
a draw to either one, then potentially you have a hand that can take
down a very big pot, as it is well disguised and you will probably get
a lot of action.

Playing Starting Hands from the Big and Small Blinds

Many players lose a lot of money from the blinds. This is usually because they play too many hands, mistakenly reasoning that since they have a third, half, or full bet in the pot, they may as well see the Flop for just a little more.

The problem is that on later rounds they are in early position, with what may be a very weak hand. My advice is to treat the blinds as middle position and play the hand following the guidelines previously mentioned for middle position. My only caveat is to raise even less frequently. Raise only with a very strong hand, as you will have to overcome your poor position on each subsequent round. Especially against multiple opponents, call and see the Flop rather than raise. Raising in the blinds rarely thins the field in low-limit games if there are a number of callers Pre-Flop and will put players on notice that you have an above-average starting hand—not ideal. If the Flop misses you and you check, you become very vulnerable to bluffs. So again play selectively, as in middle position.

In the Small Blind, look for a reason to play rather than fold. Do not slip into the habit of calling just about anything because you only have to put in half a bet or two thirds of a bet to see the Flop. If you do call too liberally, you may often find you will Flop hands like top pair with a poor kicker, and now you have a tricky hand to play from a poor position.

Taking Out the Trash

Most often you will be folding before the Flop. You will be dealt cards like J5; 10 3; 72; and the like. These hands have no straight or flush possibilities and even if they make top pair will be outkicked. If they are not in the previously-mentioned rankings and classifications, they are trash. Absolute trash. Discard them without a second thought.

Discarding trash is the most important thing that you can do Pre-Flop to provide a foundation for winning play. Playing in the way I suggest will mean that you will probably play half as many hands as your fellow players or less. That is good.

TWO CATEGORIES OF TRASH TO ESPECIALLY AVOID

It can be frustrating sometimes being this selective. I have often sat at a table for two hours without having had one playable hand. When this happens, poor hands start to look good. Two types of hands that look especially good are big cards paired with a small unsuited card such as K4 and A3 or Q6. Some poker writers refer to these as **dominated hands** because even if they **make** a hand like top pair on the Flop, another top pair with a better kicker will almost certainly dominate them. They will finish second best a lot and so lose money. Discard them ruthlessly. Similarly, two-gap hands such as 69 or three-gap hands such as 8Q should be considered trash hands, suited or unsuited, as you will rarely Flop a decent draw and may again end up with a dominated hand. Muck them, they are not worth the trouble.

I have also steered you away from small pairs (below 77). These usually only make money if you Flop a set; otherwise, they become extremely difficult to play and rarely make much money long term.

The information you have about starting hands is not complex, but at first it may seem a little tricky to handle and a lot to remember. I recommend that you play on one of the Internet poker sites that allows you to play using play money, not real money, or against a computer program and have this chapter open as you play. Refer to it as you are dealt cards, and keep referring to it until it is ingrained in your playing habits. Also read it and reread it often.

Now you know which two cards to start with, when you can play them, and how to play them before the Flop. In chapter 6 you will learn how various flops affect your play.

CHAPTER SIX

Play on the Flop

IF PRE-FLOP PLAY is the foundation of good Hold 'Em, then the Flop is the keystone: to mix metaphors, it is the junction of every hand. Poor play on the Flop will be an enormous chip drainer in the short and long runs. If you learn how to play well on the Flop, you will be well on the road to becoming an expert player.

Why Is the Flop So Crucial?

Like all poker, a Hold 'Em hand is made up of five cards. Once the three Flop cards appear, you may already have a **complete hand** or nothing at all or something in between. The *almost* good hands are the ones that lose your money in poker: poker only pays money for first place. There are no consolation prizes. This means that in the struggle to win a pot, you want to be the overwhelming favorite as often as possible. It is for this reason that I limited your starting hands to those mentioned in chapter 5. This somewhat conservative selection made you one of the favorites Pre-Flop: The Flop can change everything, however. Ace-king suited Pre-Flop is a very strong hand and should usually be bet strongly. If no ace or king appears on the Flop and you do not have a made straight or flush or a strong draw, then you have a near-worthless hand or one that needs to be played with great skill to win or show a profit long term.

You should mostly fold your ace-king suited at this point. Poor players do not recognize how a hand can drastically change in value on the Flop. Poor players become married to their glorious Pre-Flop hand, and they refuse to recognize that it has turned to goo. Like a gooey substance, they cannot let it go and either call to the River without improvement or win with it occasionally on the Turn or River, never realizing that long term they are usually playing against the odds.

Here is an example of how the Flop can change your fortunes, sometimes dramatically:

You are holding:

Your opponent is holding:

This is typical of a low-limit game in which you, following my advice, will be only playing strong cards Pre-Flop but where your opponents will often play a variety of poor cards against you. In this scenario, you are a 2:1 favorite before the Flop. Your fortunes can change drastically, however, if the Flop does not hit you. For example, if the Flop is:

$$Q\clubsuit, 9\heartsuit, 4\spadesuit$$

You have become a 3:1 favorite even though you still have no pair!

However, if the Flop comes:

$$Q\clubsuit, 8\heartsuit, 4\spadesuit$$

Your opponent is now a 3.2:1 favorite. He now holds a pair and even though it is a pretty poor pair, you have gone from being a favorite to being an underdog.

If the Flop is:

$$Q\blacklozenge, 8\blacklozenge, 4\spadesuit$$

You are now even money to win the hand, because although your opponent still has a pair, you have a draw to the nut flush and overcards.

What happens if you make a pair? Let us say the Flop is:

$$A\spadesuit, 4\blacklozenge, 2\clubsuit$$

Your top pair with top-kicker turns you into a 15:1 favorite. If the Flop were to make him a pair, too, with an eight appearing, you would still be the favorite, but now only by 4:1.

If the Flop is:

$$Q\clubsuit, 8\heartsuit, 7\clubsuit$$

Your opponent has now become a 19:1 favorite! So although you were clearly leading Pre-Flop, your hand is almost useless on the Flop. Conversely, if *you* were to Flop top two pair, you would become a 164:1 favorite!

What did we learn here? First, hands that get help on the Flop become substantial favorites over those that do not, even though these same hands were much weaker Pre-Flop. In all other circumstances, however, the strong Pre-Flop hand is the favorite and overwhelmingly so when that strong hand gets a piece of the Flop. This is why you should play strong hands Pre-Flop but rarely bet or call if the Flop does not help you. This is especially true at lower limits where you are usually against multiple opponents who will often call to the end. At least one of those opponents will get helped by a favorable Flop, and now you are playing at a serious disadvantage. That is why it is rarely worth playing overcards (with no draws) in low-limit games and why you should be quick to fold cards that get no help on the Flop, if there is any betting before you, regardless of how how good those cards looked before the Flop. This is especially true when you have two big non-pairs such as AK, or AQ.

The key point is that even though the 8, 7 off-suit is a far weaker hand, when it gets help on the Flop and the ace-king does not, fortunes are reversed.

KEY CONCEPTS FOR PLAY ON THE FLOP

The point I wish to drive home is that the Flop creates a sharp distinction between the underdog and the favorite. Poor players do not recognize this, and they stay married to the **dog** and end up mostly howling at the River as the pot is **pushed** to their opponents. *You must realize that your good Pre-Flop hands can turn into trash on the Flop.*

You want to recognize on the Flop whether you are a favorite or an underdog. Usually, when you are a favorite, you should bet and raise strongly on the Flop, and when you are an underdog, fold immediately. This general strategy is modified by only two considerations: when you aim to play deceptively in order to ensure that your opponents maximize their mistakes or when you are not a clear favorite but you have the correct odds to draw (take the Turn card) to a hand that may become the favorite if you get the card you seek.

Good poker players manipulate their opponents into making big mistakes, and by doing so, magnify their advantage and winnings. It is impractical to deal with every possible situation on the Flop. Unlike with starting hands, I cannot give you a set of unchanging rules about what to play and when. What I can do is give guidelines as to how to play in the most common situations and most important how to avoid some of the most glaring errors that constitute the major chip bleeders. With this knowledge, you will be suitably armed against all but the most skillful players, and you are unlikely to encounter such players in the low-limit game.

The Importance of the "Check-Raise" in Low-Limit Hold'em

Before I begin looking at individual poker hands and scenarios, I want you to understand the place and value of check-raising. To check-raise is to raise another player's bet after initially checking. Some people consider check-raising unethical. Such people are either inexperienced poker players or bonkers. Check-raising is not cheating, nor is it unethical. It is only another tool of poker deception, vital in low-limit Hold'em. In fact, check-raising is one of the only means by which the inherently huge positional advantages of late position over early position in Hold'em can be partially nullified. I would never play in any Hold'em game in which check-raising was banned because by taking this tactic away you effectively cripple the game.

As previously mentioned, one key feature of low-limit Hold'em is lots of Pre-Flop callers. As a player following a sound starting-hand strategy, you will have either raised (or occasionally called) with a *very* strong hand or called with a fairly strong hand. If you have a *very* strong hand, you would welcome callers, as your initial advantage means that you will most likely win the pot, and the more chips in it, the better. Since these *very* strong hands do not occur too frequently, you will often be playing a hand that while fairly strong and likely to be the leader Pre-Flop, and even on the Flop, is susceptible to being beaten by hands drawing against it.

For example, you Flop a top pair with a strong kicker, but there are two cards of the same suit on the board. This means that players with a flush draw will want to call. Your objective is to either make it too expensive to do so by betting strongly at them so that you win right there or make any draw mathematically incorrect. In a poker game such as no-limit Hold'em, where there is no limit as to how much you can bet, this is easy to do. You can **protect** your hand. You simply bet an amount that makes it statistically incorrect for drawing players to draw. If they do so, win or lose the hand, they are *losing long term* because they are betting against the odds. In fixed-limit poker you do not have this luxury: you can only bet a sum equal to the limit of the current betting round.

The combination of a large pot with lots of potential callers creates a situation in which the poor players' desire to call may inadvertently coincide with correct play. They may only be calling because they want to play, but the large pot and other callers often combine to give them the correct odds to draw to a hand, which if made, will beat yours.

Another example: you call Pre-Flop in early position with a good hand (A, Q nonsuited clubs and hearts), four players call, and the player on the button raises. The Flop comes Q♦, 10♦, J♠. Now if you bet and four players behind you call, the final player, who let's say is drawing to a flush (he holds the king and jack of diamonds), easily has the odds to make a call in the hope of drawing another diamond on the Turn or an ace, making him a straight and you two pair—a very difficult poker situation. Now you face a dilemma: by *not* betting, you run the risk that all behind you check and thus give away the dreaded **free card**, giving your opponent, in effect, unlimited odds to make a call to beat your hand.

By doing this, you create a mathematical disaster when he gets the free card and a poker disaster if he in fact draws a diamond to beat you. What to do? Damned if you bet, damned if you don't, it would appear. Fear not, gentle poker player: The check-raise, like a night in shining armor, is galloping on his milk-white steed to rescue you! In fact, the check-raise is more like Merlin than Galahad because, as if by magic, you are going to force your opponents to make poker errors. Here's how: instead of betting, you simply check. When the Pre-Flop raiser bets, as he often will, you now raise instead of merely calling the bet. If those players between you and the raiser call with any type of drawing hand, they are making mathematical errors by calling two bets, not one, as they no longer have the odds to **chase**.

You are forcing your opponents to magnify their mistakes; you are playing winning poker. If the other players fold (you have thinned the field) and the Pre-Flop raiser now calls *your* raise, he makes an error by entering a pot against the odds when you have the best hand, and thus you have made a player put money into a pot in which you are the clear favorite to win. If the original **bettor** re-raises, any other players calling two bets cold, are making errors. Hence, the magic of the check-raise.

Of course, no poker tool is perfect. In the preceding scenario, the Pre-Flop raiser could have merely checked, and you would have *given away* a free card. So if you plan to check-raise, you must be pretty sure that someone behind you will bet. When they do, your raise creates an unpleasant option with players holding weak hands. If a diamond falls on the Turn, you will probably have to fold, but if it does not, the Pre-Flop raiser's check on the Flop would have indicated weakness and you should have come out betting on the Turn, reasoning that he held a possible flush draw, with the odds to win squarely in your favor. He is making a huge error calling on the Turn now, since he must call twice the sum of a call on the Flop and only the River card can make his hand.

If you believe that there is little chance of a bet because the players acting behind you are passive, then you should bet out in the hope that some will fold, thus removing the drawing odds from players who may be drawing to flushes or straights.

So far, this has been the most complicated poker tactic that I have described. It is in fact much easier actually to do than to read about.

HOW THE CHECK-RAISE CAN WIN YOU A FREE CARD

Most players do not like being check-raised. The experience is often unpleasant and therefore memorable. If you check-raise often, you will be somewhat feared—and possibly loathed—because players will be afraid to bet into you after you have checked for fear of being check-raised. This fear and passivity will often cause players not to bet when they in fact should do so to protect their hands. This is to your advantage if *you* are the one drawing to a flush or straight because you can often *get* a free card.

THE PLACE OF THE CHECK-RAISE

Warning: you can become addicted to check-raising. This is not good, because if you do it all the time, other players will not bet, and thus you will not be able to check-raise! Like all poker tactics, check-raising must be used selectively and wisely. This is where watching and studying your opponents and the flow of the game is important: against aggressive players, check-raising is a very good method of keeping them under control; against more passive players, you usually want to bet hands that you believe are strongly leading on the Flop.

Now I will describe, in order of card value, the most common occurrence on the Flop. By following these guidelines, you will be able to handle most poker situations, and for the most part, I will keep you out of situations where difficult decisions are required. The most complex poker decisions occur at the margins of profitability. They are the decisions that only add a little to your profitability. To the expert player, the ability to make correct decisions consistently in these complex scenarios adds up to create a significant winning edge. In a game played between experts, these fine choices can make the difference between profit and loss, or most often, increase and decrease of win rate. In the Hold'em games in which you'll be playing, this is almost irrelevant, as many of your opponents will be making such gross errors that you merely have to avoid these to stay ahead of the game. You won't enjoy as high a win rate as an expert, but you will still do nicely if you maintain discipline.

A Way to Look at Flop Play

Some poker texts at this point start to go into generalized theories about Flop considerations, odds, outs (the cards that will make or improve your hand), and whether you have a "green," "amber," or "red" playing situation. Personally, I have found this to be a hard way to learn to play. Although poker is a game of odds and probabilities, it is also a game of repeating scenarios. Once you recognize the general scenario, then you have a range of actions to choose from. An understanding of odds is of course important, but the same statistical scenarios occur repeatedly, so despite what some poker writers insist, few good players are constantly calculating odds. What they are doing instead is continually evaluating each poker scenario to determine how they will act. Experience consists of the continual and ongoing evaluation of a variety of poker factors in constantly changing scenarios again and again. Odds are one key factor, but poker moves too fast and decisions have to be made too quickly for you to have to be always calculating odds.

To make life simpler and more practical, I will describe commonly occurring situations and card holdings. You will therefore have clear guidelines as to how to play in these situations, based on what holding you have on the Flop. Afterward you can calculate odds, if you wish to, to verify the accuracy of my advice, but for all practical purposes, if you follow my advice, you can quickly become a good player, even if you cannot back up all your playing decisions with cogently argued statistical evaluation. So to put it more simply, do what I say and you will be playing correctly most of the time!

How to Play When You Hold a Pair on the Flop

If the Flop, **hits you**—that is, makes you some kind of hand—the hand that it is most likely to make you is a pair. Playing pairs well on the Flop in crucial to winning poker. Pairs come in many different shades of strength. Recognizing when you have a strong pair is more than just knowing if that pair is composed of high cards or not. It depends on the other cards on the Flop, your kicker, the suits on the Flop, the number of opponents, and your position.

Fear not—despite all these factors, many decisions are quite straightforward. We will explore these together in this section, using different pairs and card holdings to illustrate each point.

These are your pocket cards:

This is the Flop:

This is a good Flop for you as you hold top pair and top kicker: the ace. However, while it is likely that you are leading at this point, you must play **fast**, that is, put in bets and raises, if others bet, right away. Here is why: This hand is vulnerable to many other holdings. If the Turn card is say a jack of any suit, it makes a straight if any player holds a king, or if any diamond falls on the Turn, it creates a flush for a player holding two diamonds. You must make it expensive for your opponents to play while you have the statistical advantage. Playing this way, you may get hands like KQ to fold as well as players holding diamonds to fold also. There is a slight possibility that you are already beaten, as many players will play the 9 10, giving them two pair. However, if you followed my advice you would have raised Pre-Flop with the AQ suited, and more than likely someone holding 9 10 would've folded Pre-Flop. Any player with KJ Pre-Flop will of course be in a great position with a made straight. I'll describe how to handle this in a moment.

If you are in early position, you should have raised Pre-Flop in an attempt to thin the field. This may or may not have worked, as many players will call one raise in a low-limit game. If the field still has four or five players taking the Flop, then this presents a perfect opportunity to check-raise. Of course, you have to be almost certain someone will bet, or you risk giving a free card to all the possible draws.

If I were in middle position and it had been checked to me, I would definitely bet. In this way I would eliminate the risk of a giving a free card to a drawing hand. If I were unlucky enough to run into a player holding KJ, I would still bet. The reason is that any player with a made straight is likely to raise back immediately because he will want to win the pot right there and avoid the possibility of **splitting the pot**, which may happen if an ace or jack falls, giving other players holding a single ace or jack a straight. By betting on the Flop and being raised, I can know where I am against a made hand. If after I bet, I am raised or re-raised, I can fold here or check and call to the River.

Some good players will re-raise on the Flop with only a draw hoping to get a free card on the Turn and even on the River, as players check to them in subsequent betting rounds. If you suspect this, you must bet again on the Turn if no card making a straight or flush falls. If you are raised, you can fold, knowing you are almost certainly beaten and that your single pair is not enough; if you are not raised, your *opponent may fold*, or if they call your bet, they are making an error by continuing with a drawing hand.

Your aim with a top pair and strong kicker is to win the pot on the Flop as others fold, or instead, thin the field so that the pot becomes a two-horse race. If your raise serves only to thin the field, you increase your likelihood of winning the pot by drawing against players who Flop two pair. By raising, if someone bets, you also punish players holding top pair but with weaker kickers. Many players in low-limit games will routinely play cards like QJ or even Q9 (and a lot worse than that) regardless of position. Very often, the Turn and River will not improve their hand, and you will have maximized your profit. So the lesson is that you almost always want to play top pair with a strong kicker fast.

Here is another classic example where a deviation from that general rule is a surprisingly sound idea:

You hold:

The Flop comes:

A bet is not bad, but here, *checking is a stronger play*. Your aim is to check-raise someone holding say KQ or KJ when that player bets. You are much safer than in the first example, too. The reason is that even if *no one* bets the Flop, the presence of the ace kicker means that you have little to fear from almost any card that falls on the Turn. In fact, your check may make your opponents think you are weak, and if an ace falls on the Turn, a player holding an ace with a poor kicker may bet. Players in low-limit Hold'em often play an ace and almost any other card and will not let their hand go once they pair the ace. If another player turns an ace and bets, you can raise. They will either fold, winning you an extra bet, or, confused, call to the River where you are very likely to have them beaten with two top pair.

Another example:

You hold:

The Flop is:

Again, you hold top pair and a strong kicker. You bet on the Flop and are raised. No card making a straight or flush falls on the Turn; you bet and are raised again. Your opponent may not have you beaten and may be trying to bully you, or he may have two pair or a set. How should you play? In a low-limit game I would check and call to the River. In this way you minimize your losses if beaten, but do not make the greater error of losing what may at this stage be a large pot because an opponent who may well have an inferior hand, but is aggressive, bets at you. By playing this way, you have turned their aggression against them. In low-limit games I would only put down top pair with a good kicker if (1) I knew that my opponent was someone who would not bluff or play very aggressively without a very strong hand or (2) A **scare card** fell, making a potential straight, flush, or full house for my opponents.

In a low-limit game, I would rarely just fold this hand. I stress *low-limit games*; in bigger games populated by more skillful players, there are other tactical considerations.

If you make a pair on the Flop and you hold a good kicker, but are unsure as to whether you are leading, check and call on the Turn and River. Since your starting requirements are likely to be more selective than your opponents', you will be surprised at how often you turn over the best hand. Many new players watch tournament poker on TV and try to duplicate the hyperaggressive play they see there. This is rarely the optimal strategy in the typical low-limit game and can be very profitable for you when playing against such opposition.

TOP PAIR WITH A POOR KICKER

Although if you follow my advice you will be playing mostly high cards before the Flop, sometimes you will Flop a pair with a medium or low kicker. How come? It usually happens because you played a suited ace (or sometimes a suited king) with the hope of flopping a flush or four to a flush (a play I do not recommend to a novice), but instead an ace falls on the Flop, and you have no draw to a flush. It can also happen when you have a weak hand in the big blind, check Pre-Flop, and find yourself with a top pair and a weak kicker on the Flop. How should you play?

Position matters a great deal here: If you are in a late position (and playing a suited ace, which you should be) and there is a lot of action on the Flop, that is, four or more players have put in bets and raises before the action gets to you, you should probably fold. You are likely to be outkicked, and coming in second or third is likely and costly. Ironically, in early position you could bet, hoping to get players with draws or top pair with a weak kicker to fold. In a low-limit game, many players will stay for one bet on the Flop, hoping to catch a card on the Turn (a poor play), so you may just thin the field or get no one dropping out. If no card making a potential straight or flush falls on the Turn, bet again to drive drawing hands out, as players now have to call the double-sized Turn bet, thus making it costly for them to continue. Once again, if you are raised and re-raised, you may want to fold. If you are raised, you could fold or call the raise and check on the River. If it is checked behind you, you have put in the same number of bets as checking and calling on the Turn and River, but instead, your aggressive action may have won you the pot by causing others to fold.

In early position, another, more sophisticated, tactic would be the check-raise. If it works, it may buy you a free card on the Turn and River and lessen the number of opponents willing to play on the Turn and River, and you may showdown the best hand.

I do not recommend that you just check and call on the Flop, Turn, and River. This is a weak play, and you will often lose to players who catch some sort of "miracle" card to make two pair or an inside straight. *Generally, you should play boldly and aggressively when the conditions are right—or not at all. This is the hallmark of winning poker, the tight-aggressive style.*

If it seems that bold play is not right given the action ahead of you, *fold.* This way you save money in a less-than-optimum situation and avoid entering a marginal poker scenario that demands complex decisions.

In his excellent book, *Winning Low Limit Hold'em,* author Lee Jones coined the term "dominated hand." This is a hand that will virtually always lose to a better hand. Top pair with a poor kicker is an example of a dominated hand, and playing such hands will lose money. Your overall tendency should be to fold this hand on the Flop, unless you believe you have a good reason to play. Top pair with weak kickers can be frustrating, chip-draining poker. Avoid it!

PLAYING WHEN YOU HAVE AN OVERPAIR ON THE FLOP

An **overpair** is a pocket pair higher than any pair or potential pair on the Flop. Here is an example:

You hold:

The Flop is:

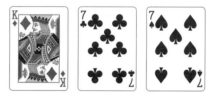

This is usually a very good Flop for you. You can beat all holdings except a player holding pocket kings or any player holding a seven. Also, if an ace falls, it may give another player a pair of aces, but you have a full house. In this case I would bet right out or raise it if there is a bet ahead of you. In a low-limit game, many players with only a king will call to the River and assuming no king falls on the Turn or River (unlikely), you will win the pot. If someone does have a seven, there is little you can do. You will probably see it to the end. You still have a draw against someone holding a seven, and you have everyone else crushed, so I would not recommend that you fold this hand in a low-limit game unless you are absolutely convinced that you are beaten.

HOW TO PLAY WHEN YOU HOLD SECOND PAIR OR
BOTTOM PAIR ON THE FLOP

It is very rarely worth betting with **second** or **bottom pair** in low-limit Hold'em. Since you will often have five or more players seeing the Flop, it is very likely that at least one holds the top pair, and with second or bottom pair and no good draws, you are way behind. You should usually check and fold, unless you cash in on the Turn to make two pair or trips. This is a situation in which you make money in the end by folding early in the hand and avoid paying off the top hand. This is exactly the opposite of how your less-disciplined opponents will play. Avoid the temptation to "see one more card."

There are a couple of exceptions where you can play second pair, but if you never do so, you are not giving up much and you are lessening your bankroll fluctuations. Here is one exception: if the pot is large and your kicker is higher than any card on the Flop, you may continue in the hope of pairing your kicker on the Turn to make two pair.

Here is an example:

You hold:

in late position. Six players call and you call.

The Flop is:

On the Flop, one player bets, one folds, and four call. The pot is large, with lots of callers, and eleven bets in the pot, with no raise Pre-Flop or on the Flop. Here, I would call because if you catch an ace or nine on the Turn, you will almost certainly take down a large pot. The pot is offering you excellent odds for this play. If you do not improve on the Turn, you should probably fold. However, if there is no raise on the Turn, but one or two people call, you can call again hoping to catch on the River. This sort of play can win you a big pot but cause a lot of bankroll fluctuation, as it will fail most of the time. You must make it very selectively, when conditions are right, and *do not* take this example as a reason to play loosely on the Flop.

When you make bottom pair, unless the conditions in the preceding paragraph apply and the pot is also huge, you should just about always fold. In fact, routinely folding when the Flop has barely hit you is sound practice.

Occasionally, you will hold a pocket pair and a potentially *larger pair will Flop*. It looks like this:

You hold:

The Flop is:

If a lot of players take the Flop, and you, of course, will have raised with the two queens Pre-Flop, you are almost certainly beaten and someone is almost certain to hold a king. This is a good example of where a great Pre-Flop hand becomes almost worthless. With no draws, your chances of making a set of queens on the Turn are only 23:1, so unless the pot is offering these enormous odds, you should check and fold if there is a bet. In a higher limit game, there are times when you could bluff at this Flop, but the nature of the low-limit game makes this an almost worthless play.

The following is an example of where making two pair on the Turn could cost you a lot of money!

You call Pre-Flop in middle position with:

The Flop is:

Here you must bet and raise strongly on the Flop because many drawing hands can beat you. If a queen falls on the Turn, you face a dilemma: your hand has improved but anyone holding any eight or king beats you. If you now see one or more players "wake up" and bet and raise on the Turn, you are probably beaten and should fold, since only another jack or queen makes your hand. *It is important to recognize what hands you do not want on the Turn and River, as well as the ones you do!*

Inexperienced players often play seemingly oblivious to the fact that some hand improvements are not to their benefit, and they continue to put in bets and raises when they have almost certainly turned from being the leader to the trailer. Thinking about what cards are good and bad for your pair on the Turn will help you avoid this type of card blindness.

The last type of pair that I want to mention is a pair with what is known as a **redraw**. Let me show you an example:

You hold:

The Flop is:

Now this is a very strong hand, as you have top pair and a strong kicker. You probably have the best hand. You should play strongly, betting and raising. If you are unlucky enough to be against a set of jacks, sixes, or deuces or two pair (yes, it is possible in a low-limit game that someone might hold, say, a jack and a six), you may still draw a heart on the Turn to make a flush. This is your redraw. Since no straight draws are possible with this Flop, you should bet strongly, and you will win the pot most of the time, whether or not your hand improves.

I have given you many examples of pairs in various combinations. I do not expect you to commit this all to memory. If you practice on the computer, you will start to recognize the types of poker situations I am describing, and you will develop a sense of how to play them. Reread these chapters between poker sessions; they will remind you of how to play correctly and what factors go into your poker decisions.

Here is a golden tenet of poker: *strive always to make the best decision in each poker scenario and do not concern yourself with the result of that particular hand.* Good poker is all about making good decisions again and again. Poker has a considerable element of luck. This means that correct actions from the standpoint of positive expectation and probability are not always immediately rewarded. This can be frustrating and disconcerting, as we are raised to believe that right actions have just rewards and vice versa. This is true in the long term in poker, but each individual hand may or may not turn out in your favor. This is where the element of luck comes into play.

This leads us to your overall poker goal, which is *to choose those plays consistently, and only those plays, that have a positive expectation.* In other words, you strive always to play with probability in your favor.

How to Play When You Make Two Pair on the Flop

There are two ways you can make two pair on the Flop: a split two-pair and a pair on the board when you hold a pocket pair. A *split two pair* is a hand consisting of cards of two different ranks in your hand, and each rank appears on the Flop. The *pair on the board* has already been discussed in the last section, so most of this section will concern a *split two pair.*

Although not a monster hand, a split two pair is a powerful holding. Much of its strength comes from the fact that it is well disguised and therefore hard for your opponents to read. You are likely to get plenty of action from players who hold only a top pair or even a draw. *You should usually play this hand fast, putting in bets and raises immediately on the Flop.*

I constantly see players in low-limit games slowplaying (not raising in the hope that weaker hands will not fold, but remain in the pot calling and thus building a larger pot) this hand and hoping to draw players in to win a big pot. This is usually a mistake. This hand is hardly ever suited to slowplaying, especially if you are following my starting-hand recommendations. Here is why: since you are usually starting with hands that are close in rank and suit, when you do Flop a split two pair, you are vulnerable to lots of straight draws and flush draws.

Here is an example:

You hold:

The Flop is:

At this point, you almost certainly hold the best hand, but any player holding a K10 has a straight draw, as a 9 or A on the Turn makes their hand. A player holding 9, 10 also has a straight draw with an 8 or a K making their hand. A player holding A10 or K9 has a draw to an inside straight. Any player holding two diamonds of any rank needs only one more diamond to make a flush. In a low-limit game, most players will draw to straights (often having the correct odds), many will draw to inside straights, and many will play any cards of the same suit before the Flop.

How should you play? Remember your aim is to win the pot right here by getting others to fold or to make it very expensive for any drawing hands to continue. If you think someone holding top pair will raise if you bet, bet out and re-raise when it gets back to you. Check-raising may be the right play, but you must be *almost certain that someone will bet*. In this situation, even the remotest possibility of giving away a free card (a potential disaster) should mean that you bet right out, hoping aggressive players behind you will raise, rather than check-raise.

If you re-raise and are raised again, you might be up against a set already. Bad luck! You will probably lose a lot of chips, but you should still check and call to the River. The pot is now probably too large to fold, and you may improve on the Turn or River. Better to be wrong for one or two extra bets than give up a large pot containing many bets. When you are faced with a choice in poker between two potential errors, choose the one where the mistake will have the smallest effect. Even if the board makes a flush or straight on the Turn or River, you will probably want to check and call to the end unless you have a very certain read on your opponent.

Most of the time, even at a showdown you will have the best hand and win a nice pot, but you must play fast. If you are against another big hand, there is little you can do, but do not make the mistake of playing weakly and allowing other players with drawing hands to catch up and beat you. Punish them by playing aggressively.

HOW TO PLAY WHEN YOU FLOP TOP AND BOTTOM OR BOTTOM TWO PAIR

In the previous example you made top two-pair on the Flop. Of course, you could make a different two pair. Here is an example:

You call half a bet in the small blind with:

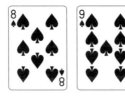

The Flop is:

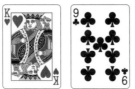

This hand is not as strong as top two pair, but it should still be played strongly. A player holding a king—especially with a strong kicker—is likely to play fast on the Flop. You must fight fire with fire! Raise and re-raise on the Flop. If a king comes on the Turn, your play is ruined, but at least it is a clear fold if someone bets. If you re-raise and get raised back, then you may be against a player holding K9 or K8. This is definitely possible in low-limit Hold'em, unlikely as it may seem that anyone should play a hand such as K8. Here again check and call to the River if no scare cards appear. By playing starting hands close in rank, you will not have to face this situation of flopping top and bottom pair too often.

How to Play When You Have Trips on the Flop

I love trips. I especially love them when I Flop a set, that is, I hold a pocket pair and I get one more of that rank on the Flop. Sets have won me enormous pots in both cash and tournament play. In pot or **no-limit** play (beyond the scope of this book), they can often mean that you double your stack, or "double through" an opponent. You will see trips, especially sets take down monster pots if you watch the televised poker tournaments. Losing to a set when you have, say, top pair can be very costly, and you cannot do much when you are faced with a set. When you make a set, you stand to win a big pot, especially if your opponents are aggressive. Why is a set such a moneymaker? Once again: disguise. If you hold a pocket pair and another of your rank Flops, it is almost impossible for even the best players to put you on such a hand. When I Flop a set, I feel like a leopard in a bush, waiting to pounce on my near-helpless prey. But I don't wait too long, and neither should you.

When you Flop a powerful hand like a set, it is very tempting to slowplay. This is usually the wrong way to play a set in the low-limit game. In low-limit games, players with all sorts of indifferent cards will stay for a bet on the Flop. Once the pot gets big enough, they almost cannot put down any hand that has the remotest chance of winning.

Given this common scenario, when you Flop a set, play fast and strong—bet, raise, and re-raise; tricky play will normally just cost you money. Sometimes, when I Flop a set in late position, I call the Flop instead of re-raising. I greedily aim to trap people in the pot and raise on the Turn. Doing this in the past has made me curse my greedy self because I have won smaller pots as players fold the Turn or allowed hands like inside straights to **draw out** on me. Do not make this mistake; play trips and sets fast. Are you in doubt? Do you want to slowplay and truly milk your opponents? Let me show you in this example why it is usually incorrect to slowplay here:

You hold, Pre-Flop:

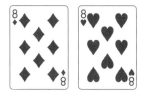

The Flop is:

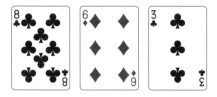

You will smile smugly (but only inside, keep your poker face) as you realize you have Flopped the nuts. You have the best possible hand at this point, but you are far from clear yet: any club on the Turn could beat you to make a flush. You are vulnerable to any 2, 5, 7, 9, or 10 that could make a straight. If any other player makes a flush or a straight, you are now a 3.4:1 underdog to improve to a full house or **quads** to beat your opponent on the River. Are you beginning to see why slowplaying here is usually a costly mistake and why you should aim to maximize what goes into the pot, *right now*? Even if your opponents have open-ended straight draws (45, 57, or 79) on the Flop, you are still more than a 3:1 favorite.

Against either a straight or a flush draw, you will win over 60 percent of the time. Therefore, the play clearly has a positive expectation, and you must maximize the advantage while you have it. This means betting, raising, and re-raising, if you have the chance. Any money that your opponents put in now is to your advantage. By raising the pot, you can effectively make it incorrect for any inside straight draws to call, but by slowplaying and only calling, you may well give your opponents both the current odds and certainly the implied odds to make this call correctly. You would effectively turn this play into a poorer proposition (even a losing one) by not betting and raising aggressively.

Now it may be that if you bet out and others call, players with an open-ended straight draw have the odds to call. In effect you are both playing correctly. If it is checked around, nobody bets the Flop, and you allow a free card to the flush and straight draws, you are giving them infinite odds (0 size pot) to draw—terrible poker. Since you have the lead and the best possible hand, everyone else is chasing *you*. This means that you have the greatest **equity** in the pot, and right now *you* benefit the most from every additional bet that goes in.

Will you drive money out of the pot by raising on the Flop? Possibly. You also increase your chances of winning, and as a pot grows, you constantly want to increase your chances of winning it. If six other players see the Flop and you call, all may call. If you raise, three may fold, but the same amount of money is in the pot. In addition, you have three less players to beat and a lower chance, therefore, of someone drawing out on you. Also, some of the players who call a double bet are probably making significant errors by doing so. The main purpose of slowplaying is to allow a lesser hand to catch up when you Flop a monster. Even flopping a top set is not a monster and would only become so if you turned a full house, if the board pairs, or another eight gave you four of a kind.

So now you may think that my diatribe has meant that I believe you should never slowplay a set. Not true! Poker is a game rarely capable of absolute rules—only guidelines. What I am saying is that if you play your set fast and put in bets and raises on the Flop, you may not always maximize your profit, but you will hardly ever be making an error. Like much of poker, and especially play on the Flop, there are exceptions when a slowplay with a set is appropriate. Here are two:

1. The pot is small and the Flop is not threatening, and you are willing to risk lesser hands catching up a little so that you can trap other players in a pot in which they have poor chances of winning.
2. You believe that you do not have the best hand.

Let me give you an example of the first scenario.

You raise in early position with pocket kings:

The Flop is:

You choose to check the Flop, and when the others bet, you **smooth call**. There is little that can hurt you on the Turn: there is no flush draw, and only a player holding 78 has a straight draw, and such a holding is unlikely to call a Pre-Flop raise from early position. You are in a commanding lead against a player holding top pair or two pair (unlikely with this board). If a player is holding a 9 or 6 and another falls on the

Turn, you may have a lot of action, as they make trips and you make a full house. Also, if one of your opponents is holding A9 or A6 and an ace falls on the Turn making them two pair, they will likely bet and raise, and you are still well in the lead. The risk may be worth it to win a larger pot, but if your opponents do appear to improve on the Turn, you must now put in bets and raises because you would hate to see a "miracle card" (say making some player a flush or straight) come on the River to beat your top set.

Every so often, you Flop a set, but strongly suspect you are beaten. This is never a pleasant occurrence, and it can be very difficult to play well.

For example:

You hold:

in last position. There is a raise from middle position and two callers; you re-raise and the other four players all call your re-raise.

The Flop is:

You have top set but it is a miserable sight. Any two clubs beat you, as do 78 and KQ. You are not facing an easy poker decision. How should you play? Last position here has a particular advantage because you may have sufficient reason to fold your hand if the action is too heavy before it gets to you. Yes, you heard right, fold top set.

Anyone with less than a straight flush or ace-high flush is likely to bet out or raise strongly because if another player holds the ace of clubs or another club making up part of a straight flush, they *must* bet out to prevent players with these hands from drawing a free card to beat them. Any player with a made straight will have to do the same to prevent any player with a single club from outdrawing them if a fourth club appears on the Turn. If there are a number of bets and raises before the action gets to you, you are almost certainly against a made flush or straight or a four to a flush or straight, at the very least. True, the board could pair, giving you a full house, or the jack of spades could fall on the Turn or River, giving you quads, but these are unlikely occurrences.

If there is one bet and a series of calls, then you are possibly looking at a made straight or low flush with the callers possibly holding the king, queen, or ace of clubs and hoping to pull another club on the Turn. In this case, you could call because the pot has become large and you are looking to draw to a full house. If all the players check, then either they have nothing or someone is holding a monster and trying to trap others in a slowplay. In either case, you have to bet, as you cannot allow free cards. If you bet and get check-raised, you could now fold, as you are just about certain to be against a made hand. Some authors may recommend that you check and call to the River, but I believe this is a poor, weak play. By betting out, you force other players to make the uncomfortable and difficult decision about how to play. I always prefer to put the question to my opponents and dominate the hand when I can. Betting with a top set may not always win, but it is hard to call it a mistake. I have to confess that only a bet, a raise, and a re-raise would make *me* let go of this hand. An old poker saw says that with a set you will either win a lot of chips or lose a lot.

The nature of this hand makes this quite likely! By betting, you are playing correctly against anything other than a made hand, and in fact, if there is a bet to your immediate right, raising may well force players with one to a flush or straight to fold, as they would be getting poor odds and they may fear that *you* have the made straight or flush. If the board does pair, your full house would be well disguised and flushes would not fold. Now although there are many considerations here, you can see that strong, decisive play is usually best. When in doubt, I tend to bet out. I sometimes lose a few chips, but it mostly puts my opponents under tremendous pressure, causing them to err. This can also help when I sometimes bet strongly on a bluff. Vigilant opponents will have seen me showdown strong hands before and may well fold mediocre holdings, compounding their errors and increasing my profits to boot.

To summarize, you are usually better off playing sets very strongly on the Flop. It is hardly ever an error to do so, and on the few occasions it is, there is probably not much you can do about it. With the few exceptions and special situations just mentioned, play sets fast and you'll often be raking in a good-sized pot.

How to Play When You Have Four to a Straight or Flush on the Flop

In higher-limit games against tougher opponents, four to a flush or straight can be a curse. It is the type of hand that in strong company may lose you a lot of money if you become attached to it, as good players will bet and raise strongly on the Flop with the deliberate intention (quite correctly) of chasing out drawing hands. However, in low-limit games, four to a flush or straight may present some of your best opportunities. Here is why:

- You frequently have sufficient odds because of the high number of Pre-Flop callers who often appear in low-limit games. This situation gives you the odds or implied odds (players continuing to call after you make your hand) to make a draw to a flush or straight correctly.

- You can often win large pots when this type of hand hits, as many of your opponents will continue to call with weak hands because they reason that the pot has become too large for them to fold.

- Your opponents' poor hand-reading skills will mean that straights and even flushes are well disguised.

- Your opponents will not give you credit for the hand unless the board is very threatening or has few other possibilities.

Another factor to consider is that since low-limit Hold'em has so many hands with multiple players and so many hands that finish in a showdown at the River, the winning hand is often much closer to the nuts than in tighter games. This gives us another irony of the low-limit game: you often need better cards to win than in a higher-limit game. How come? Well, since for any given board the nuts is rarely less than a straight, you will need better hands to win at a showdown in the low-limit game than you will tend to need in a higher-limit, tougher game because more hands go to a showdown. For all these reasons, you will find yourself playing straight and flush draws frequently in the low-limit game.

What the odds are for straights and flushes, and why the differences should not cause you to lose sleep: Some poker authorities wax lyrical about the shades of subtle difference between straight and flush draws—and far be it from me to trample on their expertise. However, while there *are some important differences between straight and flush draws* that I will describe later in this chapter, in the low-limit game they are often equivalent in terms of playing tactics. In terms of odds, you are a 2.2:1 underdog to make a straight by the River and a 1.9:1 underdog to make a flush by the River. These odds are so close as to make the playing strategy almost identical whether you have four to a straight or flush.

Now, I am not saying that all draws are the same. In fact, drawing hands can be categorized with many subtle shades of difference. While an understanding of these subtle differences will increase your winning edge, you can still do very nicely with a more basic but sound understanding. So let us view some of the more commons situations, and you will quickly see play is often straightforward.

COMBINED FLUSH AND STRAIGHT DRAWS

I do not know if there is a poker heaven, but if there were, this would be the type of hand that the truly worthy would have in that big low-limit game in the sky. Now I suppose in heaven, you would get aces all the time, your opponents would never remember and bet, and you would win just about all the time—but where is the fun in that? Combined straight and flush draws are very strong hands, and in the earthly low-limit game they can bring you a lot of lucre. Let us start with a monster draw:

You hold:

The board is:

Oh my goodness! It doesn't get much better than this for a drawing hand! This is an open-ended, straight-flush draw with twenty-one **outs** to top pair or better. If this type of hand does not get you excited, then, dear reader, you are indeed a cold fish. Although even against a large field you will win with this hand over 50 percent of the time, you should still *not* slowplay it. Put in bets, raises, and re-raises on the Flop. It could be that all may fold and you will win a moderate pot, or some may call. Your only real fear is against a set, which could improve to a full house. Yes, it could happen, but hey, this is gambling, and here you are doing well to play fast and strong on the Flop. In the low-limit game, you will not lose many players, and they will often have inferior hands and draws. Your opponents will be drawing to lower straights, flushes, and two pairs (which can make you a straight), or they may hold top pair with poor kickers. Keep playing strongly and only fold at the River if you do not improve. If the board pairs on the Turn, you would check and call with this type of hand, but plan on going to the River. Okay, that was too exciting! Let us calm things down a bit with a slightly less exciting but more common scenario.

A flush draw:

You hold, in last position:

There are five callers and no raise, and you call. You could also raise Pre-Flop here, which would be a strong play but would likely cause more fluctuations in your bankroll. However, a call is just fine (as recommended in chapter 5), and you get the chance to see a Flop with very good odds.

The Flop is:

Now this is a good Flop for you, even though at present you have no hand. You have one **overcard**, but more important, you have a draw to the nut flush. You are a little less than a 2:1 underdog to make your flush, so what is your goal? You want to have at least three other callers with you, to give you the correct odds for a call to see the Turn. In a tougher game, a player holding a jack will bet, and maybe another holding another jack will raise, making your call marginal. However, in the typical, passive, loose, low-limit game, you will probably not lose anyone here, as many will opt to see "just one more." This is good for you. If someone raises immediately before you and others have called, you should still call the double raise as the previous callers will often call one more bet. With all those bets in the pot, you are making money every time a poorer drawing hand or weaker pair puts in a bet.

If, in fact, you choose to raise on the Flop in last position, you may well find that all the other players check to you on the Turn. You should check too, giving you a free card (well it cost two bets on the Flop) on the Turn and a look at the River as well. Of course, if the flush does fall on the River, you may not get many callers, but you will still win a nice pot.

In this type of drawing situation, when you are drawing to the nuts, you want to encourage others to stay in a pot. This gives you correct odds, builds you a pot, encourages others to stay in, and provides a satisfying pot, if you win.

Here is an open-ended straight draw:

You hold:

The Flop is:

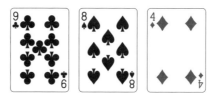

You hold two overcards to the board, but more significantly, you have an open-ended straight draw. Also, there is no flush draw possible on this board of three different suits, known in poker parlance as a **rainbow** board. You have sixteen likely outs (although a jack on the Turn or River may make someone else two pair or give him top pair with a better kicker) and should encourage your opponents to call by not playing too fast and continuing to call in order to have sufficient odds to see the Turn and maybe the River. Your play should be almost the same as if you were holding a flush draw, as just described.

Look out for the double **belly buster**! Straight draws are sometimes so well disguised that even when you hold one yourself, they can be hard to see. One such example is the double **gutshot** straight draw, otherwise known as a double belly buster. Two *inside straight draws* are combined to give the odds of an open-ended straight draw. If you do not look at your hand and the board carefully, you may miss this opportunity, believing it to be an inside straight draw only, which you muck, because you believe you have insufficient odds to make a call.

Here is a double belly buster:

You hold:

The Flop is:

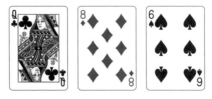

At first glance, this looks like an inside straight. In fact there are *two* inside straights; a jack or 7 will give you a straight, both giving you the nut straight. You should therefore treat this hand like an open-ended straight and bet or raise accordingly. This is an extremely difficult hand for your opponents to read, and in confusion they may well give you a lot of action, calling your bets and raises liberally, especially if your opponents hold top pair, with a strong kicker. When this hand holds up, it often wins a good-sized pot. Look out for these opportunities.

SHOULD YOU DRAW TO INSIDE (GUTSHOT) STRAIGHTS?

I do not have the advantage of an American upbringing. However, I am given to understand that one shibboleth of poker wisdom passed to ensuing generations of young men is ". . . son, never draw to an inside straight."

Very good advice if the standard game is the stuff of Westerns—that is, Five-Card Draw—as you almost never have the odds to make this play correctly. But we are talking about Hold'em, a game unknown to the Old West, not Five-Card Draw. If, on the Flop, you have an inside straight draw, then you are an 11:1 underdog to make the straight on the Turn. The nature of low-limit Hold'em with lots of callers, who may call one raise, may mean that there are twelve small bets in the pot on the Flop. More likely, there are fewer though, and this is where the implied odds become relevant again because if you do make your straight you will probably be paid off liberally. And again, your hand is hard for your opponents to read. If I were drawing to the nut straight, I would be willing to make this draw if I could get odds of at least 7:1 and my opponents were not that aggressive. Also, I would prefer to make this a call from late position, where a re-raise is less likely.

Now, do not overdo this, as calling with what is still a pretty weak draw is a certain chip bleeder. Be less inclined to draw if you are *not* drawing to the nuts or if there is three to a flush on the board, as it is galling to make your straight while one of your opponents makes a flush with the same card. I would just about *never make* this draw if I were drawing to the low end of the straight.

SITUATIONS WHEN YOU SHOULD BE CAUTIOUS IN DRAWING

Do not draw to straights when there are three cards of a single suit on the Flop. Almost invariably, someone is drawing to a flush, and probably most of your opponents are willing to call a double raise, especially if they are holding an ace or king of that suit. You will rarely be able to bet them out of the pot, so I recommend that you check and call to the River. If the action on the Flop or Turn is heavy or if the fourth card of the suit falls, fold.

If there are three cards of the same suit, you can bet or even raise with the nut-flush draw, but with anything else, it is wiser to check and call. Again, if there are many bets and raises, you are almost certainly looking at a made flush. In this instance, only the nut flush is worth continuing with, as you may be against the nuts already if you are not drawing to it. Even if you are drawing to the nuts, you want to have at least two other players in the hand to make this play worthwhile. It is a poor mistake to call a bet if only one other player is in the hand and the pot is small, even if you are drawing to the nuts. This type of draw is not profitable long term, when the pot is small.

Avoid draws when the board is paired. Again, check and call or fold if the action is heavy. An opponent may have a full house or be drawing to one.

THE VALUE OF DRAWS

The draws mentioned provide great opportunities to win big pots in low-limit Hold'em. You will tend to have more of an opportunity to make this play correctly in the low-limit game than in bigger games. You will also appear to your opponents to be a gambling sort of player because you call and raise with draws. This image tends to ensure that you will get a lot of action, is essential to decent profits, and is hard for your opponents to read. Also, making a big draw (when you have the odds or implied odds to do it) is great fun. I especially like it when one of my opponents has slowplayed his big pair Pre-Flop and Flop and allowed me to continue with a draw because he greedily wished to slowplay and trap me when he should have been betting and raising to prevent me playing on. Winning this type of hand when you make your draw is very satisfying, particularly against the "expert" at the table who looks on your hand with withering disdain. "How can you play those cards?" he asks in disgust.

"Gee, just my lucky day I suppose," you smile as you somehow rake in another large pot. To them, you may appear a reckless fool. You will know why you acted so.

How to Play When You Flop a Complete Hand

Ah, joy of joys! The Flop comes, and you immediately have a straight, flush, full house, or even four of a kind. What to do when such a happy event occurs? Let us ascend the ladder of complete draws together and see.

You hold:

The Flop is:

You have a straight but you must *not* slowplay! Put in as many bets and raises as possible, as you want to make it as expensive as possible for any player holding two spades to draw to the flush. If someone has flopped a set, or the low ("ignorant" in poker parlance) end of a straight, you will get lots of action, and at this point at least you have a commanding lead. If you are in last position and there have been callers ahead, raise, do not merely call. Your hand is not enough of a monster to slowplay. If another player is on a big draw or has a set or two pair, he will not fold, regardless of the raises you put in. Some players make the mistake of waiting for the big bets to start hitting hard and heavy. This is a mistake. You give draws a cheap chance, and you do not maximize your advantage. Bet, raise, and re-raise, as long as you believe you have the best hand and force others to chase you.

You may lose a few players, but you will make it very difficult for players with weak flush draws to call so many bets and raises. If a player with a poor flush draw folds and a spade does come on the Turn or River, you may save yourself a pot by betting heavily here and pressuring them to fold. If they choose to continue and the spade does *not* fall, you have a big pot, and they have lost lots of chips. Of course, a player with a set will continue, despite pressure, and probably should. He is hoping to "**fill** up" and make a full house. If the board pairs on the Turn, slow down! Check and call to the River unless you face a re-raise, then you are almost invariably beaten. The same advice applies if the spade falls and suddenly others bet and raise. You are probably looking at a flush. So in summary, play made straights hard and fast on the Flop, and only fold if the board becomes very scary and there is a *lot* of action on the Turn or River.

Here is a made flush. You are in early position.

You hold:

You call, there are four callers, and the button raises. You call the raise.

The Flop is:

This is a great Flop, but again, play fast. As a general rule, the bigger the pot gets, the more you want to do to win it straightaway, if you have the lead, but are at all vulnerable to other hands. In this situation, you could try for a check-raise, but personally, I would come right out betting with this hand, hoping that the button raises with say, an overpair, and I get a chance to re-raise. True, everyone may fold to my initial bet, but I have still won a decent pot. A tricky slowplay in which I merely call would allow any player holding the ace of diamonds a correct draw to the nut flush, and I would have egg on my face if I allowed this to happen. Of course, there is a slim chance that I am against the nut flush already, but I should still play strongly on the Flop. If I get a caller, who then raises or re-raises on the Turn if *no* diamond falls, then this player either is very good (unlikely) or has the nut flush. Here I would check and call to the River because the pot is so big. If he does not have the nuts but a lower flush than mine, I make a big mistake by folding. *Better to make a mistake for two big bets than to give up a pot that contains ten or more bets unless you are certain you are beaten.*

If *you* Flop the nut flush (you hold the ace), then you can call the Flop and start swinging hard on the Turn and River with raises and re-raises. However, if there is a raise and re-raise on the Flop, raise again, as you do not want to give any player holding a set a draw at a full house. *The bigger a pot gets, the less concerned you should be about disguising your hand and the more you should be concerned about doing whatever you can to win it right there.* I would only put down the nut flush if the board paired twice. I recommend you do the same!

Flopping a Full House

You will be dealt a pocket pair one time out of every seventeen hands. About 1 percent of the time when you have a pocket pair, you Flop a full house. If you hold two cards of different ranks, you only have one chance in a thousand of flopping a full house. Yes, this all happens rarely, but when it does, how sweet! When you Flop a full house, you hold an absolute monster. Now your only real concern is how to play to maximize your winnings. You stand almost no chance of being beaten. This is where you *should* slowplay because you want to give other players a chance to improve their hands and make them believe they have a chance to win and thus continue to put in bets and call raises. Here the feigned weakness of a slowplay is appropriate to draw players in, especially if the pot is small. When I Flop a monster like this, I usually just want to call any bets or raises on the Flop. I am hoping that some player improves to a straight or a flush, because I will get a lot of action out of them and I am almost guaranteed to win a big pot. Again, the only caution is not to take this too far, because it can cost you money. I have seen some players who are so intent on being tricky that they forget to bet. They wait to trap on the River, and the only response they get is a lot of folding. If no player has raised on the Turn, you should raise with this hand and you should usually re-raise if there has been a raise. Remember, your goal here is to maximize the size of the pot. Not all full house Flops are the same though.

Let me show you:

You hold:

The Flop is:

These are great opportunities to slowplay and wring every bet you can from the pot. Follow the advice I just gave, and pray that at least one of your opponents makes a flush on the Turn. If the spade comes, you could try to check-raise on the Turn, but better to raise or re-raise a bet if you can. You want to maximize the pot!

With a weaker full house, here your set is lower than the paired cards on the board:

You hold:

The Flop is:

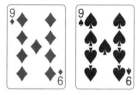

This is still a very good Flop for you, but you are vulnerable to hands such as 9J or QJ or KJ or AJ because with those hands, if a queen, king, or ace falls on the Turn or River, you will lose and will have to pay off many bets. I would bet, raise, and re-raise *on the Flop* and check and call if a queen, jack, or ace falls on the Turn and River. I flopped a full house recently when holding a pair of sevens. Two jacks accompanied the seven on the Flop to give me sevens over jacks. I had one opponent on the Flop. He bet out, I raised, and he re-raised. I raised back and he called. The Turn was a five. He bet out, I raised, and he re-raised, and I raised again (I did not figure him to have J7 or J5, a hand called "Motown" in poker circles). He raised and I raised again (unlimited raising is allowed in most casinos when just two players contest a pot), and he called.

I still felt pretty confident. The River card was an ace. I felt rather sick now, especially as he bet right out. I was now pretty certain he held AJ. If I had X-ray vision, I would have folded, but with this many bets in the pot, I had to call, because if I was wrong and he only had trip jacks, I would be making a colossal mistake. I gave him a **crying call** and of course he flipped over the AJ. Now I could wail about the injustice of being beaten on the River, and he certainly got lucky, but I could not really complain. He played aggressively with three jacks and a top kicker. I would have done just the same, except not re-raise as often as he did. He won a huge pot. Would I play differently in the future if the same situation occurred? No. I did what I could to maximize my advantage, but this time luck favored him. You have to accept this if you play: poker is a game of skill with a strong element of luck. Skill takes the money in the end, but when bad luck hits, the "end" can seem a very long way off and a lot of lost chips down the road.

If you Flop a full house but suspect you are beaten by a higher one, you should probably call to the River, proceeding with caution. In a low-limit game with players willing to stick around with all manner of crazy draws, it is usually unwise to fold before the showdown with this huge holding.

To quote from *Hair*, "When the moon is in the Seventh House and Jupiter aligns with Mars," you will Flop quads. Well, I cannot guarantee it, but it is so rare that it might as well be the case. If you have a pair and two more of the same rank appear on the board, you have a great hand, but you probably won't get much action, unless someone makes a full house. The only question for you is how to get others to play; being beaten is a nonissue. My advice would be to follow the same criteria as when you Flop a full house. You may get lucky and have some players pay you off, but surprisingly this type of hand rarely wins a big pot, as it looks too scary to other players.

If you Flop a straight flush—aah, forget it! Do what you want. Please. You're going to win, okay? Unless, of course, they have a *higher* straight flush, and then—wait a minute: Am I nuts? The chances are *so* slim. Look, if you Flop a straight flush, play it any way you want and send me an e-mail—and if you get beaten send me 10 percent of the jackpot! Deal?

What to Do When the Flop Misses You

In this seemingly endless chapter, I have tried to cover just about every playable situation on the Flop. Of course, these are only guidelines, as each situation has individual subtleties, which cannot all be covered. Only playing experience will reveal these, but keep the guidelines always in mind and do not stray too far from the path of poker righteousness if you want to keep winning chips.

The unhappy truth is that most Flops are not favorable or only mildly so. You will Flop bottom or second pair, three to a flush, or one overcard. Here is how you should play any hand or draw not already mentioned: *Fold.* Yes, that's right, *fold.* Do it now. Yes, *now.* Did you do it yet?

Do I sound like a nag? I hope so. The biggest mistake that poor players make on the Flop is continuing with marginal holdings. Don't do it! Remember, a big part of winning play is *knowing when to fold.* Pre-Flop and Flop are usually the best times, because you have either nothing or little invested in the pot, and on the Flop, you have seen most of the hand. If you are not leading, or have a very good draw with the odds, get out. Good players like to dominate or get out, and you cannot dominate if you continue weakly just to see another card. This discipline is key to winning play, and winning is a lot more fun than loose, money-draining, devil-may-care play.

I have covered just about any playable situation on the Flop. Follow these guidelines and you will be well on your way to winning play. Consistently sound play on the Flop is the surest way I know of to become a winning Hold'em player.

CHAPTER SEVEN

Play on the Turn

I F YOU ARE still with me, you are well on your way to becoming, in theory at least, a solid Hold'em player. I have already covered the most challenging and complex parts of the game. Also, some aspects of play on the Turn have already been mentioned, so sit back and enjoy this chapter. Generally speaking, play on the Turn and River is simpler than play on the Flop. Now remember, I am talking about *low-limit* Hold'em. At higher limits, play on the Turn can—and will often be—very subtle, devious, and bemusing to the less skilled. Players who play well on the Turn are to be feared. In pot-limit and no-limit Hold'em, play at this juncture and its mastery are important to your success, but in low-limit Hold'em, an altogether more straightforward strategy is not only all that is required, but it is almost invariably more appropriate.

One of the central themes that I have been stressing throughout the book is the desirability of making money by taking advantage of the grosser mistakes of poor players. The grossest mistake that poor players make on the Turn is continuing to call bets "just to see another card" and thinking things like, "Golly, if I've gone this far, I might as well call the River too, just to keep 'em honest."

Poor reasoning. In low-limit Hold'em, as I've said, you will frequently have to show down your cards at the River to one, two, or three opponents—and often more. Since this is the case, you will usually have to showdown the best hand to win a pot. Generally, then, I want you to *bet aggressively when you think you have the best hand on the Turn* and call only with good draws where you have the odds. Not too difficult, right?

"Ah but surely," you object, "this will make my play so obvious, no one will call down my hands and I'll scare everyone out of pots, and cost myself money."

Yes, you will lose a few bets like this, but in a low-limit game, you will rarely want for callers and *you must punish callers mercilessly by betting at them when you believe you are leading; also, you must protect your good hands by forcing drawing hands to call bets and raises.* When I am in a pot, I like to dominate and make players dance to *my* tune—I do not want to dance to *their* bets and raises. I will only vary from this general strategy to trap players when I have a monster hand or when I am trapping an overly aggressive player. You should do likewise.

Avoid Fancy Plays in Low-Limit Hold'em

I approve of reading—well, I am an author—and I believe in a sound poker education, but some players get a little too influenced by what they read and, especially, what they see on televised poker. They read about and see these wondrous and unusual plays and look to emulate them at the casino in a low-limit game. When this happens, they can fall victim to a nasty case of *fancyplayitis.* My poker medical dictionary tells me that this is an infectious brain bacterium that *"has the effect of deluding players into believing that the more sophisticated (fancy) their play gets, the more money they make. This pernicious bacteria has them checking good hands when they should be betting, making bluffs against players who will just about always call, and raising with weak hands to fool players (who hardly know the value of their own hand, let alone other players') into believing that they are holding much stronger hands than they are, and so their opponent will fold. The symptoms of the illness include the frequent ejaculation from the patient of remarks such as:*

"I can't believe he called my raise!"

"How can anyone play that hand in that position?"

"How can you beat people who play this badly?"

and other such absurd and pitifully illogical statements. The effect of this sickness is a prodigious bleeding of the chips and a sickly looking bankroll.

So what does the gentle and goodly Dr. Myers prescribe for this unsettling condition? Repeat the mantra "sophisticated plays fail against poor players" one hundred times a day and read passages of Myers' book twice a day until cured. So generally, play straightforward from this point onward in the hand and you will avoid the galloping malady that is *fancyplayitis.*

Let me get give you some examples of specific plays on the Turn:

You hold:

in last position.

Three players called, you raised Pre-Flop, and all three called the raise.

The Flop is:

A player in early position bet; everyone called; you, correctly, raised, and all the players called your raise. Now there is a fair chance that at least one player is on a flush draw and maybe even on a straight draw, and probably one player has a pair of tens. In a low-limit game, players with ace, king and ace, or queen may still be in the pot too, so you must bet to protect your hand. Now if a spade, queen, king, or ace falls on the Turn, how should you play? If there has been no bet when it reaches you, I would bet. Follow the general rule on the Turn to *bet hands that stand little or no chance of improvement and check those that do.* Why bet and risk a raise when you may now not have the best hand? Well, it is not an easy decision, but my reasoning is that any player holding the preceding cards will bet because he does not wish to lose a bet on the Turn and therefore is unlikely to risk losing a bet by check-raising.

You may well *still* have the best hand. Also, by betting you make it hard for players who are drawing (if no spade has fallen) to continue and players with top pair but a weak kicker to continue too. They may believe that your strong play Pre-Flop and on the Flop means that you have a hand stronger than a pair of jacks and that you have now a set, an overpair, or possibly two pair. If players now fold, *even if now you do not hold the best hand, by thinning the field, you increase your chances of winning by limiting the competition and possibly drawing another jack on the River.* Of course, if everyone folds to your bet as the scare card falls, you win.

When scare cards come on the Turn, I tend to bet or raise *if I have position on my opponents and there has been little action.* This is aggressive play and may seem counterintuitive, even reckless, but I believe it puts so much pressure on your opponents that the weaker and more passive will crumble. Of course, if you get raised or re-raised or both playing this way, you can probably fold with a clear conscience, knowing that you are almost certainly beaten. If you only induce calls, you can check on the River if your hand does not improve, and because of the strength you have shown on the Flop and Turn, you may not have to call a bet. To check on the Turn when a scare card falls (unless it makes *your* hand and you intend to check-raise) shows weakness and encourages your competition to bet at you and bluff at you to make you fold. As long as you believe you have the best hand, continue to bet on the Turn.

In trying to determine whether you have the best hand, you must gauge your opponents' actions and reactions as well as look at the cards on the board. It is a mistake to be so conservative as to believe that you are always against the nuts. If you are up against an opponent who will never bet until he holds at least top pair and you know that he plays in this way, you could fold to a bet from such a player on the Turn. It is also a mistake to believe that others are constantly trying to bluff you out of pots. Most players are far more timid and bluff less than you might think.

Should You Stay with Drawing Hands?

If you have a draw to the nuts, or at least a strong draw, the Turn will clarify your decisions as to whether to continue. Here is an example:

You hold:

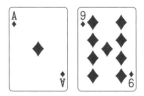

on the button. Five players have called and you call too.

The Flop is:

One player bets the Flop, two call, two fold, and the action is on you. You decide to call—a little loose, but not a bad play given the action and the possibilities. Let's see how various Turn cards will govern your play:

If an ace falls, you have two pair and can raise the bet, as your only slim fear is that another player has an ace and ten to make a higher two pair. Still, *you* have a good two pair and a draw to the full house. If another nine falls, you can raise any bet as you have trips, should another diamond fall, you can call if there is a bet, as you are drawing at the nut flush. Any other card makes a fold a pretty straightforward decision.

Not all draws on the Turn are playable. If the board pairs, it is time to fold. If you are drawing to a straight and a third suited card appears on the Turn, your draw is just about valueless, so you can fold to any bet.

When to Play Aggressively on the Turn

Earlier, I cautioned you against overindulging the slowplay. The more solid play is to bet and raise strongly on the Flop, with the exceptions already mentioned. This is not the way many of your opponents will play, however. They will slowplay the Flop and wait for the double-sized bet on the Turn to show aggression, hoping that they will win a larger pot. This will of course cost them bets and give other players the odds to draw out on them, so this is good for you. By contrast, *your* aggression on the Flop will often mean that players check to you on the Turn—very useful when you are drawing yourself—and when you get a free card, it means that you are getting unlimited odds for your draw. However, *you must continue to bet strongly on the Turn with any hand that merits it.* Don't try to be too cute by going for fancy check-raises, as you may miss bets. If you check a strong hand on the Turn and there is no bet and you come out betting on the River, only very weak players, or those who want to showdown their hand because it is strong, will call. Overly fancy checking on the Turn when you have a strong hand may give your opponents' drawing hands a chance, and this is not good. If you have decided to see the hand through at this point, play strongly and dominate, or fold. This is the type of tight-yet-aggressive play that is the hallmark of the strong player. Follow my advice, and you are on your way to becoming one.

WHAT TO DO IF YOU ARE RAISED ON THE TURN?

Being raised on the Turn is never comfortable. If the Turn card is one that is likely to make another player a strong hand, you can probably fold. It is easy to see this if the board pairs, a third suited card falls, or a card that makes a straight falls. The hardest situation to read is one where the Turn makes another player two pair. The question you need to ask is, is the Turn card likely to do this?

For example:

You hold:

The Flop is:

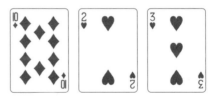

You bet the Flop and are called by one player.

The Turn card is the nine of clubs. Since you still have top pair with a strong kicker and there are no flush or straight possibilities, you confidently bet out and your sole opponent immediately raises. Now you have a dilemma: does he have nines and tens, a common starting hand, or was he merely slowplaying the Flop with a hand like ten and jack or ten and queen? This is where observing player tendencies is invaluable. You would have to ask yourself questions about this player, such as:

- Would he start with this hand in this position?

- Would he play this hand against only one opponent?

- Is he a player who habitually slowplays the Flop?

- Is he so conservative that he would only bet if his hand improved?

Of course, however well you read hands and opponents, it is all speculation to some degree because many players do not play consistently. Still, the process of deduction is valuable. If you're very sure that your opponent would only bet with two pair, you could fold or you could call and check and call on the River, the latter being the more conservative play. Personally, unless I were absolutely certain he had two pair (and there I may well fold), I would do neither; instead, I would re-raise! "Madness!" you say. "Why risk another bet if you may be beaten?" Here is my reasoning (which, gentle reader, you may criticize, pointing out the flaws of my logic in petulant epistles if you wish): If my opponent does have two pair or stronger, he will surely re-raise, and then I can fold with a clear conscience, and it has only cost me one bet. If he only calls, I can check behind him at the River if I do not improve or bet if I do, winning a larger pot. If he does *not* have two pair, but was merely slowplaying, then this re-raise puts a lot of pressure on him. Whether I win or not, he will know that I will be feisty on the Turn and hard to bully, so he may be less inclined to try for a slowplay in the future and be less inclined to raise me on the Turn. I concede that my play is very aggressive and will fail against a very tight player, but it stops the audacious, and the sneaky, cold. This type of play throws your opponents into temporary confusion and sets the seed of uncertainty. Sometimes my own deviousness shocks me! Of course, I am describing a more advanced play, so you may wish to check and call hoping to win at the showdown, but bear this example in mind when watching others play and consider its effect.

In conclusion, continue with your strong hands at the Turn, unless you have compelling evidence that you are beaten.

CHAPTER EIGHT

Play on the River

A T THIS POINT in the hand, play is normally the most straight-forward and the need for disguising your hand has just about disappeared. In pot-limit and no-limit games, play on the River can be very difficult, frustrating, nerve-racking, and challenging. This is rarely the case in limit, and especially low-limit poker. If you have come this far, you are probably going to see the hand for one more bet unless you have a busted draw or the River convinces you that your hand is now absolutely worthless.

However, a number of important considerations and concepts have to be grasped to play this part of the hand well, and not understanding these will lessen your profit considerably and drain your chips unnecessarily.

How to Play When You Believe You Have the Best Hand (or a Very Strong Hand) on the River

If you have been leading out with the betting at each juncture of the hand, don't stop now. Bet! A consistent error I see is that some players mysteriously stop betting on the River, even though they have been betting all the way through the hand. This seems to be a result of some confused logic about "beaten opponents not calling and only better hands calling bettors at the River." This twisted logic is based on a misunderstanding of a valuable concept I shall cover at the end of this chapter.

In low-limit games, opponents who have come this far will tend to call with almost any halfway decent hand. If you do not bet, you allow people to check hands such as second pair or top pair with poor kickers, and thus you do not visit your righteous and complete poker vengeance wholly upon them. The indiscipline of poor players should cost them royally at the end when you make them pay for playing a hand that they should have mucked Pre-Flop.

If you do not bet when you believe you have the best hand at the River, then you cost yourself a lot of money over time. This is especially true if you make your drawing hand at the River. In low-limit games, if you make your flush or straight at the River and believe it to be the best hand, bet and do not attempt to check-raise. Even if you think someone else will bet, you should still bet—then you have the option to re-raise if someone else raises. This can make for a very nice pot when an overly aggressive opponent attempts to bully you when you, in fact, have the stronger hand.

How to Play Marginal Hands in Big Pots

In low-limit Hold'em, where many players are calling and staying in the hand, pots can contain many bets by the River. Now, if you have followed my advice about starting hands and playing the Flop and Turn and you have any sort of hand outside of a busted draw or perhaps a lone high ace, you are probably going to have to call. You have a hand that you felt was worth continuing with to the River, and now the pot has probably gotten large with perhaps as many as ten or more big bets in it. With a good, but not great hand, your choice is now to make a mistake for one big bet by calling or make a mistake for the whole pot by folding. I would prefer to make a small mistake rather than a big one.

Some players like to look like experts at the table by making the big lay down at the end. They are, in effect, saying that "I can read your play and your hand so well that I *know* I am beaten and I will demonstrate my knowledge by majestically folding."

I have seen this type of playing, especially from the resident table expert, a frequent character in low-limit games. This type of player will snort at bad plays, lecture others on poker theory, and ridicule opponents' play. He, as a self-proclaimed expert, is capable of making the big lay down at the end.

In an Indiana riverboat casino one night in a low-limit game, I bluffed one such player three times at the River when a scare card came down. He was the sole opponent and three times he folded, allowing me to win combined pots of over $375. His ego would neither allow him to be beaten at the end nor showdown a holding that did not conform to his concept of correct play, so he folded, glowering at me, as I had obviously put another bad beat on him. I figured that if even one bluff succeeded, I would show a handsome profit on the play. Because all three did, it was rather pleasant.

I then realized that he started to believe that I might be bluffing, so in the next pot when I was against him and a third suited card fell—giving my ace and queen suited the nut flush—I showed a little hesitation before betting out in an overstrong manner. His eyes lit up briefly, as he realized that at last he had caught me in a crude bluff and prepared to smite my presumption summarily. He raised. I immediately re-raised and sat back in my seat. His ego again did not allow him to be intimidated by a rank amateur like me (especially one with an English accent), and he promptly re-raised. I must confess to a little Hollywood acting at this stage, where I tried to show a combination of concern, fear, and thought (pure fantasy, as I had the nuts), and after this show, I, of course, re-raised. The expert called, showing a respectable king-high flush, and when I turned over the nuts, he was almost apoplectic with rage—but he couldn't complain about a bad beat. He went into a sullen sulk thereafter and left the game a little later mumbling something about how he couldn't play "real poker" against such fools (actually "fools" was not his precise description of his playing companions).

I was only mildly sorry to see him go. His boorish behavior was upsetting other players and lessening my enjoyment and chances of winning. So do not be afraid to make a smaller mistake by calling at the end rather than folding with a good-but-not-great hand that may well take down the pot. And this leads me to the next topic.

Raising Wars at the River

In the last section, my sole opponent and I got into a raising war, and since the casino allowed unlimited raising when only two opponents were left contesting the pot, we could conceivably have raised and re-raised away our whole stacks. How does one handle a raising war? Well if you have the nuts, no problem: just keep re-raising—but you must make sure you *really* have the absolute nuts, or you may find the raising war a costly exercise. When playing in a pot-limit game (on the Internet) a short time ago, I had the incredibly good fortune to make a straight flush on the Turn, a very rare event. How could I extract the most money from the remaining two opponents? Well, of course, my best hope was that someone had the ace-high flush, because hardly anyone will ever put you on a straight flush—understandably, given its rarity. I checked from early position, and sure enough, the first player bet the pot (you can do this in pot limit) and the next player called—strangely to my mind—and then I called. My thinking was that if the first player had the flush, he would bet again on the River, allowing me to raise. The River card paired the board; I checked and the first player bet the pot. To my joy, the next player raised the maximum. It looked like he made the full house. Now of course, I *could* raise the maximum, but the first player would definitely fold, so I just raised a small amount. The first player called my raise, and the next player put all his chips in. I then raised **all-in**, and the first player folded, thinking that he was facing (correctly) at least one full house. Of course, I won the showdown, and the player with the full house was very unlucky to run into a straight flush, but they both made the mistake of very strong betting (they bet most—and in the case of the second player—*all* his chips) with less than the nuts.

I, too, have been overaggressive at the end when I have gotten tired, thus careless, and did not see that a flush was possible when I had, say, a straight and found myself in an ill-conceived raising war. Look carefully at the board to make sure you have the nuts.

Many times you will have a strong hand and not have the nuts, and yet you may get raised on the River. Then what? Again, you should almost certainly call. If you have the nuts, you still may have to split the pot. This can happen when the board is say, six, ten, jack, queen, king, with no flush possible. Any player holding an ace will split the pot with a straight. Some players just check and call if they figure that they are going to split the pot with one or more other players. This is a mistake. I have seen some players continue to call with less than the nuts, for example, with the low end of the straight, and I have on rarer occasions actually seen players with the nuts fold to a raise, because they misread their hands and did not properly read the board. *If you have the nuts at the River, raise as often as allowed; you have nothing to lose and may win more than you think.*

Maximizing Your Winnings in Multiway Pots on the River

In low-limit Hold'em, it is often the case that three, four, or more players will see their hands all the way to the River. Since this is the case, it is not always obvious how to play to maximize your chances of winning. For example, you have been drawing to an ace-high flush; there are four players still in the hand on the Turn. On the River, you make your flush and you now have the nuts. The first player bets and you are next to act. How should you play? You may think that this is obvious; since you now have the best hand and there are no more cards to come, you may as well raise. Maybe not. Remember, at this stage you have won the hand; the only question is how to maximize your winnings. If you raise, the two players behind you will probably fold, as will the original bettor. Your raise will have only gained you one large bet. However, if the pot is large enough, all manner of hands may be tempted to call, so if you call rather than raise, you'll make more money if only one of the players behind you calls. If you get really lucky, one of those two players may actually raise, and then when the action gets back to you, you can re-raise.

Another factor to consider is that the more players in the pot at the showdown, the closer to the nuts the winning hand will be. Marginal hands lose much of their value in multiway pots at the end if they do not make the nuts. Say, for example, you make a straight at the end, but there are also three suited cards out, or you make a flush, but it is not the nuts. If there are more than two people contesting the pot, you should prefer to call rather than raise, even if you are pretty convinced you have the best hand, but *not* the nuts. This way, you can still win more than one big bet at the end, but you are risking only one. By raising, you risk two big bets and may win only one or get re-raised by a player holding the nuts or any better hand. So at the end, you want to ask yourself two seemingly contradictory questions:

1. How can I maximize my winnings?

2. How can I limit my risk while doing so?

You have to make a judgment as to whether calling or raising at the end will give you the best chances, and this decision is based on your hand, the betting, the nature of the other players, and your assessment of their likely holding.

When you bet at the end with what you believe to be the best hand to maximize your winnings, you are said to be **betting for value**. In low-limit Hold'em against players who call too much, you should definitely bet for value more often. However, *you should only bet at the end if you figure to have the best hand most of the time when you are called*. This concept applies to marginal hands on the River.

Suppose you're holding:

in the Big Blind. There is no raise and you check. The Flop gave you top pair and the final board reads:

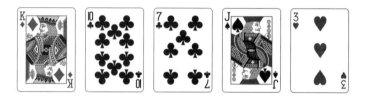

You bet the Flop having top pair and to prevent giving flush draws a free card, and you bet the Turn too. At the end, two players remain. What happens if you bet the River? Well now, any busted flush draw will fold, and the only player likely to call is a player who has made top pair with a better kicker, or perhaps two pair, at the Turn. So you may gain nothing if you bet and may well lose an extra bet if you are called because only players who already have you beaten are likely to call and showdown. In other words, your bet has no value. In this instance, since you are *not likely to have the best hand when called, you check.* If someone bets into you after you check, you should call, but this way you only risk one bet with this marginal call. So when betting or raising on the River, ask yourself: "Is my opponent likely to call my bet or raise with a worse hand?"

If you think not, check—the bet has no value.

When in doubt, bet at the end if you believe you have the best hand, but think about these concepts carefully if you want to maximize your winnings and build a foundation to better play.

PART THREE

Reading the Game and Reading Your Opponents

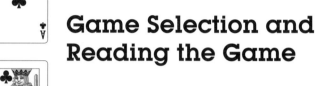

CHAPTER NINE

Game Selection and Reading the Game

UNLIKE MOST CASINO games, poker is played against other players, not the house. With other table games and with casino machines such as slots, the house makes its money because it has a built-in percentage advantage. With the exception of Blackjack and possibly a couple of other casino games, this percentage advantage remains consistent. The long-term effect of this advantage is that the longer you play such games and the more money you wager, the more you will lose. It's designed that way. Casinos are in the entertainment business, and they offer comfortable, safe, congenial, and reasonably fair environments for adults to indulge the need to take a chance.

Casinos don't gamble. In return, sometimes you get the opportunity to walk away a winner because short runs of luck may favor you. The casino does not mind this at all, as long as you do not cheat. In fact, winners are good for business because they encourage others to gamble. The built-in percentages that favor the house are regulated either by law or by competition, but the casino knows that a few fortunate winners will barely dent the profits made from the majority of losers. It is on such percentages and notions that huge gaming empires are built. When you put your chips down at most table games in a casino, *you* are gambling, but the casino is not. In gambling parlance, the house usually "has the best of it."

Poker is quite different. The casino makes its money either by charging a fixed fee to each player for every half hour or hour played or by taking a small percentage from each pot, known as the rake. The casino does not care who wins or loses. What it wants is for the tables to be fully active for as many hours as possible: more players, more time charges or rakes, more money. It does this by creating an environment consisting of comfortable and safe surroundings, fast and friendly dealers, considerate management, scrupulous monitoring of the games to ensure that no players or dealers are working in concert to cheat others, and attractive waitstaff who will ply you with drinks and snacks as you play. Some casinos even offer back and neck massages at the table! The casino also tries to spread the most popular games at a range of stakes, so that everyone who enters the poker room to play can find a comfortable, enjoyable game.

Casinos have something of a love-hate relationship with poker players though. Poker rooms turn a profit for the house, but nowhere near as much for the space occupied as table games or slot machines. The casinos know that when an unsuspecting novice sits down at a table of poker sharks, he will usually lose money fast. This money goes to the more skillful players and not to the house. The money that a patron might have lost in days at blackjack, craps, or roulette can be gone in a few hours at the poker table, and the house sees none of it. This is why poker rooms are often somewhat obscurely placed or hidden away in many casinos.

Poker is a game where the less skilled will lose to the more skilled over time. I am a fairly good player. If I sit down at a table with nine less-skilled players, I will take all their money over time. Not all at once; not necessarily fast; but if we continue to play together, they will surely lose, because *poker is essentially a game of skill with an element of luck.* Conversely, there are many players better than I am. If I were to sit at a table with some of the world's best players, I would probably lose all my money to them in a short time, luck being equal. This means that if you want to win consistently, you must ensure that you are one of the best two or three players at any table you sit at. When I made a third of my income at poker, I was very careful to ensure that I was one of the best at the table. Hell, I had bills to pay—this was a part-time job! I remember looking at higher-stakes games for a long time and realizing that I was not yet ready for them. I was outclassed.

Now, the aim of this book is not to turn you into a high-stakes, professional player. It is to enable you to have fun at a casino without losing your shirt and to make a tidy profit over time. However, if you want to have a good time, I strongly suggest you do not play beyond yourself. So how does one go about selecting a good game in which to play, and how does one recognize good players? After all, unlike athletes, poker players don't have any special look. For most of us, a few minutes' perusal will lead us to the conclusion that we could not hold our own against a professional tennis, basketball, golf, or football player. Their skills are obvious if we watch them play for a few minutes. How do we spot competition that is too strong for us at the poker table? For the beginner this is not easy, but after reading this and the next few chapters, you will know what to look for, what games to sit in, and what to avoid.

Warning! These concepts are important! Ignore them at your peril!

Some players wholly undervalue or only pay lip service to the importance of game selection and identifying player types and game characteristics. They spend hours analyzing play and too little time analyzing the playing environment. If you follow my guidelines, you will not make similar mistakes. So read on if you want to win and have fun.

Game Selection: Why Some Games Are Far Better Than Others

The presence of poor players in a game generally makes the game better if you are more skilled. In fact, even the presence of one fish can make an enormous difference to the profitability of a game. Some players maintain that too many poor players in a game make it unplayable. This is nonsense. What it tells you is that the player who says this does not know how to vary his game to take advantage of this fact; this is a common failing among players who do not give sufficient thought to matching their playing style to current game conditions.

In poker, we make money from others' mistakes. The grosser these mistakes and the more money they put across the table in making them, the more money we stand to make. A quick theoretical illustration: imagine that a table consists of ten players all the same level of skill. Let us call this skill level A. What will happen if they play together? Well, not much. They will pass money between each in turn, being up a little or down a little as luck changes and the cards run. Now let us substitute two of these players for two others of a lower skill level, level B. Certainly, the B-level players will enjoy runs of success, but as the game continues, they will give up more and more of their chips to the level A players until they are out of chips.

The level A players will take a roughly even amount from the level B players, effectively sharing the level B players' stake among them. This will not happen in one session or even over a few, but over time the B players will surely lose. Their presence in the game has greatly increased the profitability of the game for the A players, and their absence makes the game unprofitable. This is of course a highly simplistic illustration, but the essential point remains valid. In chess tournaments, players are given a rating based on how they play against each other. As you gain victory over more highly rated players, your rating number increases. At the highest levels in chess, it is no contest for a Grand Master to play against someone two hundred points lower than himself. The Grand Master is certain of victory, because chess is a game of pure skill not luck.

The rating system saves hopeless mismatches and ensures that players play against others close to them in skill level, thus avoiding the boredom of almost inevitable victory or defeat. No such system exists in poker, and the element of luck often means that in the short term poor players can appear to be much better than they are because luck allows them to win pots even when they are consistently outclassed. But not forever. Over time, luck is pretty evenly distributed and skill wins out. You cannot ask a poker player, "What is your rating?" By the time you realize you are hopelessly outclassed, you may have lost a lot of money.

Generally speaking, poorer players are to be found in lower-stakes games. This is not always the case of course, but most players as they begin to win consistently and dominate at a level like to move up. This is a natural poker progression. Since this book is aimed at novices or near novices playing at low-limit Hold'em, these skills are more than enough to win consistently at most games up to $10–$20 stakes. Beyond that you will need other skills outside the ambitions of this book. So when cutting your poker teeth, the first thing to do is to start in lower-stakes games. Try a $2–$4, $3–$6, or $4–$8 game to start, regardless of your current level of wealth. I am told, though I do not know if it is true, that Bill Gates, the world's richest man at the time of this writing, enjoys $3-$6 Hold'em in the casinos, even though he could comfortably buy several casinos. He doesn't need the money. He gets his fun playing at this level when he wants to play. If you are not a professional, why on earth do you want to play if not for fun? Be wary of slipping into the ego challenge and adrenaline rush that comes from playing in a game where a loss (or a win) could substantially affect your lifestyle. Playing in games that are too high stakes or too difficult will create a lessening of your ability to play solid poker. You will be "scared money," as the saying goes. Remember, have fun! Winning is fun! Winning happens when you play well at a comfortable stake, against slightly inferior opposition. Since most players at low-stakes poker do not read books like this and you do, if you read and apply what I say, you will be above average for your stake level.

CHARACTERISTICS OF THE IDEAL GAME AND GAMES TO AVOID

Now I would like to give you some thumbnail pointers that indicate a game is ideal, at least for someone with basic skills:

1. *The game has a low enough stake. (See previous section!)*

2. *The game is full.* Do not sit at a game with less than eight players. If

you have to, do so for only two dozen hands or so until the game is full. Do not sit in a short-handed game (less than five players). I love shorthanded poker. I have won some nice money at it, but most players, especially newer players, are not good at it. It demands a reevaluation of your hand holdings, new skills, lots of aggression, plenty of moxie, and a bankroll large enough to stand the invariable fluctuations. It took me about three years to become good at shorthanded play, and I lost lots of money at it before I did. Even now when I play shorthanded, I want to be pretty sure my skills are much better than my opponents', or I leave the table. Avoid it for now.

3. *Games in which there is a lot of calling but not too much raising Pre-Flop.* I will talk more specifically about this later in this chapter, but for now, look for these more passive games. If every hand is raised and re-raised, leave the game. You will play fewer hands, your bankroll will fluctuate wildly, and you will feel stressed and uncomfortable. Look instead for a game in which on average three to five people are seeing the Flop and the bet has not been raised or if so, only once. Lots of Pre-Flop raising may indicate the presence of wild players (**maniacs**) or better players who have stepped down a class. *You are looking for a loose-passive game.*

4. *Avoid games in which there appear to be drunken players.* Drunks lose money, but they slow down the game and are often obnoxious. Who needs that?

5. *Avoid Games with very few Pre-Flop callers or the "**rock** pools."* They call them **rocks**—tight (selective) but essentially passive players. They are not dangerous, but you cannot make much money from them, and they are boring to play with. The archetypal rock is the retiree who uses the poker room as his social club. Players like this are very conservative and wait for a few premium hands before they play. They only continue if they have an excellent holding and rarely bluff. They usually enjoy small but steady wins,

but make for a very dull game. Rocks can be easily beaten. I will talk about this later in chapter 10. If you play on a weekday afternoon, you can expect to see quite a few rocks among the regulars. The tables they play at have little raising, few players seeing the Flop, and very few at the showdown.

6. *Avoid games with excessively high pot rakes or time charges.*

7. *Monitor the game you are in.* When you sit down, watch the players' actions. See if certain players are calling almost every hand or staying too long after their hand is clearly beaten; see what cards they showdown. Each game will have its own flavor and characters. Generally, you are seeking a fairly passive game, with little aggressive raising; moderate but not minuscule pots; and one in which the players appear to be having a good time. Avoid tables where the players seem to be arguing a lot or seem excessively glum. Also, be wary of tables where one or two players have very large stacks of chips and the rest have very small stacks. Through either luck or skill the game has moved in their favor, and the remaining players may well tighten up and thus make the game unfavorable for you.

GAME SELECTION: PRACTICAL REALITIES

I have given you a whole host of guidelines to help you determine if the game you are playing is beatable for your level of skill. You will see similar advice in other poker books, and it is good advice: practical reality may differ, however. A personal anecdote if I may: When I was a young poker lad, still fresh from the computer simulators, I was determined to try out my new-found knowledge in one of the temples of poker. The particular temple I chose to make my pilgrimage to was the Taj Mahal; no, not the one in Agra, India, but its garish and gaudy namesake that sits in stately, if overblown, repose on the boardwalk in Atlantic City. At the time (and possibly today), this casino belonged to that well-known shrinking violet, Donald Trump. It boasted the largest poker room on the East Coast, and possibly the world. So I felt sure that it would be easy to find a game of my choice in both limit and style. I took the bus from Port Authority in New York City, and some two and a half hours later, I found myself in said emporium of gambling.

The poker room is not hard to find, and having dispensed with my coat and bag at the cloakroom, I wandered over thinking I could just take a seat. Oh dear. Yes, the tables were busy and there were lots of them. So busy, in fact, that I and several hundred other poker hopefuls had to put our names on a waiting list for our chosen game. About one hour later, I was called. It felt like I had won a prize. I had the privilege of sitting in an indifferent game with a bored dealer, two men who looked the worse for wear (I later found out that they had taken their seats on Friday evening and had not been to bed yet), two old codgers who looked liked they had been exhumed that morning, and a youth who was disguising his age behind a baseball cap pulled down tight and a pair of mirrored sunglasses. My seat was between two middle-aged women, who in girth would not have looked out of place in the front line of any NFL team. Now this was far from the ideal game, apart from the social aspects of it, but I was not going anywhere for the day. I had *my* seat.

Poker writers who live their lives in Las Vegas seem to forget about those of us who do not when they write about game selection. In Las Vegas there is usually a huge choice of games spread at casinos all over town, and if you are friendly with the management, you can even have a seat locked up for you by phone, while you amble down to take it. I know one player who had a private arrangement with certain poker room managers in a casino to call him if known fish were present in a game and the game looked good.

In most smaller poker rooms, you usually have to accept a seat in what may be one of only two or three poker games at your limit spread in that room. There isn't much of a selection. If you want to play, this is it. In some casinos that stand in majestic isolation such as Foxwoods in Connecticut, you have no choice but to accept their game conditions as they are.

When on my honeymoon in Southern California, and against my wife's forewarnings and better judgment, I decided to visit the local tribal casino. It did not exhibit the majesty of Foxwoods. The dimly lit room was contained in what looked like a disused aircraft hangar, and milling about were a sorry group of people who looked like they had just cashed their social security checks to play. With anticipation, I asked for the poker room. Unfortunately I was directed to a dark corner where a few sullen souls played Seven-Card Stud and Hold'em at two tables. However good these games might have been, I did not intend to settle into this cave for a few hours of cards. It was too grim. I mouthed a silent prayer to the gods of poker for the blessings of Atlantic City and left in a hurry. Anyway, what on earth was I thinking playing poker on my honeymoon!

So should you give up on game selection because you may not have many games to select from? No. What you should do if you have a limited selection is sit down and monitor the game, and if it exhibits too many of the undesirable characteristics already mentioned, leave. Remember, you are there for fun. If it ain't fun, leave and do something that is. Professional players have to sit in all sorts of games. You don't. If conditions do not seem right, or you feel uncomfortable, leave.

Personally, I can do fairly well in most game conditions, unless I am outclassed. I will not continue to sit at tables where people are blowing cigarette smoke at me, where players are abusive to others or the dealer, where the dealers are either very slow or utterly incompetent (most dealers are well trained, friendly, and well managed), where players have very small stacks (no money for me to win), and where there are more than three maniacs (not the psychotic, but a player type I'll describe in chapter 10) in the game. Other than that, I'll play at just about any game at my chosen limit.

THE EBB AND FLOW OF A SESSION

You must be attentive to the flow of the game. New players entering a game can change it radically, and if you do not watch carefully, you will find yourself in a game that has become unfavorable. In the

Tropicana in Atlantic City one Saturday evening, I started playing in a fairly sedate game. I was up about $60 in a $5–$10 game, and reckoned I would leave in roughly half an hour. When it was almost eleven o'clock, three players left and three slightly intoxicated men replaced them. They started raising and re-raising every pot, and the game became wild. Within fifteen minutes I was down $200. In the next half hour I was up $100. I was mesmerized by this game now, and at two in the morning when only six players remained, I was down $100 having been up as much as $800. In the final hand I had a pair of twos. I was on the button and by the time the action reached me, the wild three had capped the pot. At that point, I was so tired and emotionally drained that I just called—a mistake. The Flop made me a set of two, but I never had the chance to bet. It was capped before it got to me— ditto for the Turn and River. I cannot remember what they turned over, but I know it was not aces, kings, or queens. My set held up, and stupefied with emotion and fatigue, I dragged in a monster pot. All I had done was call. I had sufficient presence of mind to leave the game shortly after that. Due to inattention, I had been suckered into a maniac's game, and I could have easily booked a heavy loss. Moral: pay attention and leave if the game becomes uncomfortable or unplayable for your skill level.

WHEN TO END A SESSION

So when should you leave? Well, when I was playing in Atlantic City, that was easy. When the last bus left for New York, of course! Naturally, for some of you non–New Yorkers who actually have cars, this may not be practical! Personally, either I leave when the game declines or I am fatigued and starting to make poor decisions or I have something better to do. It never has anything to do with whether I am up or down. If you are a winning player, you will come out ahead eventually. The more hours you play, the more you will win, but the fluctuations inherent in poker mean that you will sometimes exit as a loser *for that session*. This attitude constantly frustrates my wife. When I have a nice profit, she is anxious for me to leave and also to cut my losses by leaving when I am down. She believes that I must leave when ahead.

"Why are you still playing?" she asks.

"Because the game is still good," I reply. I'll stay as long as it is good, meaning I am still better than the opposition and the action is still good, with lots of money flowing across the table.

The two biggest mistakes I observe are by players who are patently outclassed and either refuse to admit it or do not recognize it and players who are playing badly because they are tired and have played for too long. Players who are tired, play worse and worse without recognizing that their play has declined. One of my favorite strategies was to play early on Sunday morning in Atlantic City. Some of the players had been playing all day Saturday and into the wee hours of Sunday morning. Sometimes they were actually sleeping between hands. Needless to say their game was not the sharpest, but very profitable for me.

In short, never let poker interfere with the need to do things that are more important or the desire to do things that are more enjoyable. Poker is a fun and challenging game, but it is only a game, unless it is your livelihood. Never let poker disrupt your family life or your enjoyment of life's other pleasures. Poker should season life, not replace it.

WHY YOU SHOULD PLAY IN A CASINO OR PUBLIC CARD ROOM

I have played in games in poker clubs that skirted the bounds of legality. I played in these clubs because they were well managed and clean and because I did not always want to make a long trip to Atlantic City. No cheating, that I could detect at least, was ever present at these clubs, and in some ways, they were a lot more inviting than the big casinos. Despite this, I would strongly recommend that you play poker in a casino or public card room if you are playing for more than nickels and dimes. Poker clubs, if not scrupulously managed, can be dangerous and rife with cheating. Casinos and poker rooms are licensed, regulated, and safe. They have a deep interest in ensuring that the game is clean and safe because they want you to return repeatedly and because they want to build their reputation as a good place to play. They have no interest in cheating you, and they wish to remain in good standing with the licensing authorities.

Never, *ever* play in games run by criminal organizations, however congenial they may superficially appear. Even if you can get out with your winnings, there will be great pressure on you to return whether you want to or not. The games will probably be poorly run, the rakes will be high, and the temptation may be great to borrow money at exorbitant rates to stay in a game that is played at stakes above your head. Criminal organizations run poker games in many major cities. Leave them to the criminals. If you live in a state in which gambling is not allowed or there are no card rooms, do whatever you can to enlighten your state legislature as to the benefits of legalized gambling. Like drinking alcohol, people, in my view, will gamble whether legally or not. Gambling is a very powerful human urge. Better to do it in a safe and regulated environment.

CHAPTER TEN

Player Types: How to Identify and Handle Them

I N HIS EXCELLENT book, *The Psychology of Poker*, psychologist Alan Schoonmaker gives a long and detailed description of player types and explains how different players' motivations for playing poker give rise to playing styles and tendencies. He also describes how to play against different playing types and styles. This information is invaluable for the professional and high-stakes player. However, unless you intend to become such or have an abiding interest in human psychology, it is probably not worth your time analyzing player types to this degree. It is certainly worth identifying broad player categories though and learning how they affect a game. This is what I will describe now.

Observing Your Opponents

A typical poker game involves a lot of repose. You normally find yourself folding hand after hand—especially if you play in the manner I suggest—and when you do find a playable hand, you often have to fold halfway through. Between hands, the dealer is shuffling, dealing, and exchanging chips, and people are entering and leaving the game. You spend only a short time playing hands. What should you do in these lulls? Some people listen to music over headphones, the more productive knit socks and scarves, and some snack and drink. *You should watch how other people play.* In fact, watching how people play is a very valuable and indeed an essential use of your time. Though people do not always follow the same playing style for each hour they play, most people tend to play within four broad and well-accepted styles. They will vary these a little depending on their emotional state, whether they are winning or losing or how tired they become or both, but they will not vary a lot. These styles of play are tied not only to a person's understanding of poker but, often, to much deeper character traits, conscious and unconscious. Only highly disciplined students of poker will be able to change these tendencies to a significant degree, and we shall discover that there is in fact only one truly desirable style.

Ignore entirely how people *talk* about their play; watch what they, in fact, do. I knew a shy and quite engaging gentleman who played with the reckless abandon of a crazed lunatic. By contrast, one player who was loud and obnoxious and possessed a boorish and hectoring personal manner played mostly passive, weak poker, but talked a great deal about raising and re-raising. It was pretty easy to bully the latter out of a pot, whereas the former might re-raise you on a complete bluff holding no hand and no draw. So I repeat: *observe how they play,* not *how they talk about how they play.* The contrasts may completely surprise you.

I am not sure how it originally arose, but it has become acceptable in poker circles to describe players by where they fall along the intersection of two stylistic axes. The first is the axis that goes from loose to tight, and the second is the axis that goes from passive to aggressive. Of course, we are only describing styles of play, not tendencies to drunkenness or other social proclivities. So in broad terms, a player can be defined in his playing style as being either "loose-passive" or "loose-aggressive" or "tight-passive" or "tight-aggressive." By loose, I mean a player who will play far more starting hands than is optimal and who will continue with them far beyond the point where he should in a hand. A tight player will play fewer starting hands and tend to fold earlier. A passive player will tend not to bet or raise but will call a lot, and an aggressive player will do the opposite. Now you have the four categories that will define the four extremes of play.

Loose-Passive Players

Sometimes called **calling stations**, you will find games that largely consist of players like this tend to be the best games. Players of this type, regardless of how they describe themselves, are inclined to be in the majority in low-limit games. They like to gamble on a hand if it is not too expensive. They believe that the game is mostly luck anyway and will regale you with stories of how they saw old Harry take down a monster pot last week with two and three off-suit when he flopped a full house. "Any two cards can win," is their motto, which means that they will play lots of hands, call one more bet on the Flop, "just to see what happens," and keep calling through the hand even to the end with a second pair, bottom pair, and worse, on the grounds that they want to keep the bluffers honest.

This player rarely raises, but will call a raise. He has come to play cards, not fold. He wants to gamble, and he wants to see if Lady Luck is smiling on him tonight. Do not try to bluff this player out of pots; he will usually call. A game with lots of loose-passive players is the best game for you. You can be aggressive without too much fear of encountering aggression, and you will get action on your good hands. Straightforward poker will win out against the calling station, and tricky, deceptive plays should be avoided. Since this type of player does little raising, you are happy to have him seated on your left because he is unlikely to raise or re-raise you.

Loose-Aggressive Players

This is the archetypal maniac. He plays lots of hands, but he likes to bet, raise, and re-raise with them. He bluffs constantly. This type of player is profitable but awkward to play against. He will win money fast and lose it fast too. He will give you a ton of bad beats. You may take all his money eventually, but your bankroll may go through some wild fluctuations in the process as he caps every round and comes from behind to **steal** a pot from you on the River against the odds. Even seasoned pros dislike playing against this type of player because if he has a lucky night against you, it can cost you a lot of chips.

If you find too many players like this in your game you have two choices: leave or tighten up a lot. And if you do the latter, fasten your seat belt—it's going to be a bumpy night! This type of player and this type of wild game is very difficult for beginners to handle. My advice is to find another game if three or more players are playing like this. If you want to ride out the storm, then play only JJ, QQ, KK, AA, and AK Pre-Flop and only continue if the Flop hits you or there are no over-cards to your pair. This makes for very boring, if profitable, poker and is not much fun. You'll be folding hand after hand if the game becomes wild and yet watching crazy hands take down big pots.

You want aggressive players like this seated to your right if possi-ble—then you can see their bets and raises coming, and you can fold your mediocre hands if they get involved in a pot. If you find an ag-gressive player to your left, try to get the next seat available that places you to *his* left.

Tight-Passive Players

I mentioned the rocks in chapter 9. They tend to be older, more con-servative players. This player is extremely selective in his starting hands, but he knows that "even a great hand can be beaten," so he calls rather than raises Pre-Flop with the hands he does play rather than throw money around. "Let me see a Flop first," he says, "then I'll tell you if I have a good hand." It is hard to make much money from rocks, although they can usually be bluffed out of pots fairly easily. If they come out firing on the Flop, fold all but your best hands. Their weakness is that their play lacks deception and fire, so you know when they bet that they must have something. They do fairly well in low-limit games, and people who are beginning to improve as players often go through a weak-tight phase first.

If you play in the morning or afternoon, you will find that many of the regulars are rocks. Too many rocks in a game make for a dull time, but two or three of them do not present much of a problem.

Tight-Aggressive Players

This type of player is truly dangerous. You should aim to become this type of player. This is solid play, selective yet aggressive. When this player enters a pot, he tends to dominate. He causes others to freeze when they should bet and call when they should fold. He knows the odds for each play, and he has carefully observed each player's style. This playing style has to be practiced because it blends two opposing characteristics, namely, control and aggression. Controlled selective aggression is usually the mark of the professional fighter. Most really good fighters disguise their true intentions, and likewise, tight-aggressive players are hard to spot because they appear to be doing contradictory things—and in a sense, they are. Like professional killers, they are in it to win and that means they want to start with an edge. There is no fair fight for them and no prisoners. Only winning. You must look at how they play: if they play few hands, but play them aggressively, raising early, folding midway through if the cards are not kind, and winning mostly when they do get to a showdown, you are looking at the hallmarks of a tight-aggressive player.

If you spot more than two players like this in your game, you may want to find a new game. Ignore how people behave! See how they play. I have seen happy, laughing poker killers; obnoxious, loud ones; and sullen, quiet ones. Ignore the exterior and look at the play. The rest is façade, and in the case of a tight-aggressive player, it is probably a practiced façade.

What I have described are extremes. Very few players will be *exactly* like these archetypes. Think of them as the stock characters of poker. Watch your opponents constantly, especially when not in a hand yourself. What cards do they showdown? From what position? Did they call a raise or a double raise cold? Do they ever bluff or check-raise? Ignore how many chips they have and examine the quality of their decisions.

In New York, I played regularly against one woman who was a fairly good but obnoxious player. She was rude, curt, whining, arrogant, insulting, and abusive. And those were her good points. She was an excellent bridge player and had a somewhat condescending attitude to us poker louts. She had a strong belief in her own playing ability and believed that she could play more starting hands and "outplay" people on the Flop and beyond because she believed she was smarter than most of us. Since she played too loose Pre-Flop, I liked to play solid hands against her and check the Flop, even when I flopped a top pair and better. When she came out betting, I would check-raise or check-raise on the Turn. She would become apoplectic with rage when she lost a showdown or folded. As the evening wore on, her play—and her behavior—would get worse and worse. By the end of the session, her play had often degenerated into loose-passive against me or weak-tight as her emotions got the better of her. Needless to say we were not friends (in fact, only her boyfriend liked her, and I am not sure even he did), but she helped me pay a lot of bills. She seemed highly aggressive, but her playing was actually mostly loose and passive.

By contrast, a quiet, mild-mannered fellow who was also a regular was a stone-cold killer. I almost never seemed to win a big pot or any pot against him. He could not be bullied out of a pot and rarely lost a showdown. When he got hit by a bad beat, he betrayed almost no emotion and he never seemed to lose his quiet, even temper. Whenever you were in a pot with him, you were nervous about what to do, as his play could spin your head. In my earlier days, I even checked a pair of aces down against him to the River. He was so aggressive that I was convinced he had a set on the Flop. In fact, he rightly put me on the bullets (two aces), and I passively allowed him a free card on the Flop and River to attempt what in fact was a flush draw. I won the showdown, but I had essentially been outplayed.

Everybody is somewhere along this spectrum of extremes of looseness and tightness and passivity or aggression, but only the tight-aggressive style is a learned style. It is *not* natural. It is borne of study, thought, and deliberate attention. By reading and practicing the style of poker in this book, you will start to become a tight-aggressive poker player. When you do, you will become a fearsome player, and I for one won't want to play with you!

PART FOUR

Miscellaneous
Concepts

CHAPTER ELEVEN

Unusual Formats, Money, and other Useful Tidbits

How Much Money Do I Need to Play?

Mason Malmuth, the prolific poker author and someone who offers some of the sagest and most practical advice on poker, has written extensively on how large your poker bankroll should be for any given level of play and win rate. I would urge you to read anything he has written on this or any other poker topic. Before we delve into what he has said, I recommend dismissing a few errors in your thinking that may be there and that I have observed in many a poker player.

NO BANKROLL IS LARGE ENOUGH IF YOU ARE A LOSING PLAYER

All recommendations regarding size of bankroll work on the assumption that you are beating the game. That even if your win rate is small, you are winning over time. The sad truth is that most players are *not* winning players; they are *losing* more or less constantly for all the reasons of bad play and game selection already mentioned. If you cannot beat the game you play in, you will lose all your playing bankroll eventually. Of course, this will be interspersed by some happy wins and possibly long winning streaks, but you will lose in the end. The simple reason is that poker is a game of skill. If you repeatedly place yourself in poker situations that have a negative and not a positive winning expectation, you will eventually lose everything, even if you occasionally "beat the odds." The last few chapters describe a style of play that will take the money in most low-limit games and make you a winning player.

YOU WON'T WIN EVERY SESSION

That being said, there is a strong element of luck in all poker games. This means that you can play well yet still have losing sessions and sometimes several losing sessions in a row. I would stress that if you have more than three losing sessions in a row you reassess your game and ask yourself some questions such as:

- Are you playing too loosely, both Pre-Flop and Flop?

- Are you playing when tired or fatigued?

- Are you steaming?

- Are you playing in games that are too tough for your current skill level?

If the answer is yes to any of these questions, correct it!

One of the hardest things in poker is to book a loss. That is to leave the tables as a loser for that session. I have stubbornly, and wrongly, played for hours, trying, in less than ideal games, to make up losses I accrued within minutes of sitting down. Don't do this. The way to think of poker is as one long session that begins when you sit down for your first game and ends when you shuffle off this mortal coil, or at least play your life's last poker game. It is all one long game. Viewed like this, a single session does not amount to much.

The only thing you can ultimately control is the decisions you make. Forget about winning and losing; focus, instead, on making the best poker decision you can, given your skill and knowledge in each situation. Forget about the last hands you played; they are history. Forget about the hands you will play, and focus on the situation *now*. It is the only reality. Focus on making good poker decisions, and as surely as night follows day, you will win over time.

RECORD KEEPING

To help with this long-term focus, I suggest you keep records of each session, the stake, how long you played, and what you won or lost. It may take a few hundred hours of play before you can determine if you are a winning player, but if you are, what you should see is a steadily climbing bankroll. There will of course be a number of losing sessions, but over time your total winnings will increase, sometimes in fairly dramatic jumps and other times much more slowly, but they will increase. Do not be too inclined to move up to bigger games too fast, and do not delude yourself into believing that you have "become a player" just because you have a few good sessions. Instead, let your winnings indicate when you are ready for the next level and be cautious.

So how much to bring? That depends on win rate and bet size. In a $3–$6 Hold'em game, a win rate (after rakes and tips) of $4 per hour would be good, $8 per hour very good, and $12 per hour or two big bets, exceptional. "What? So low?" you ask. Yes. Now, you may have a winning session where you win a lot and losing sessions too, but these averages balance out. When I made a portion of my income playing poker, I had many sessions where I won hundreds of dollars and losing sessions where I lost that much too. In a $4–$8 game I made about $12 per hour on average and in a $5–$10 game about $15. How do I know? I kept records over thousands of hours of play. Most players who do not keep records, do not remember, or often exaggerate, their winnings and forget about their losses. They think they win much more than they do. Record keeping reveals the truth.

After a while, playing felt like punching a time clock. There were of course very large fluctuations, but over time this average bore out. If I wanted to make more money at this level, I had to either improve my skills or play in a weaker game, but basically play longer to win more. Poker has some very bad short-term runs, even if you are beating the game. So what was my total bankroll for my $4–$8 game? $2,800. Now that may seem excessive, but Malmuth's writings bore this out as the sum I would need to prevent the possibility of going broke, and who am I to argue with Malmuth? He offers some very sound advice and describes his calculations in arriving at this figure.

Did I need all that? No. In fact, the worst I was ever down was $1,300, very uncomfortable I assure you, but remember I was playing to pay a few bills. I could not afford to go bust. I could certainly have lost $2,800 and still been a winning player. Professionals cannot afford to go bust. Money is their stock in trade. They must have a bankroll large enough to withstand the losses that must happen at times in each game. Playing underfunded is what causes most aspiring pros to bust out. They play in games above the capacity of their bankroll to stand adverse runs.

So am I saying you need $2,800 to join a $4–$8 or $5–$10 game? No. Not at all. This would only be the case if you were planning to play poker for a living, were a winning player, and wanted to have enough not to go bust, ever. I was effectively a self-employed player. I needed a capital base of $2,800 to fund my business to allow me to make the measly income of about $12 per hour. Of course, as I increased my stake, I played in bigger games and earned more. Actually, I never put more than $500 of my own money into the game. I had a good start in the beginning, but I was hopelessly underfunded when I started and was fortunate not to bust out. I never touched my winnings until I had over $3,000 and only took out 50 percent of my winnings over that every month. The rest went to building my bankroll until I had a playing bankroll of around $12,000. This allowed me to play $10–$20 games comfortably and to play the occasional $15–$30 game if conditions were right. If I slipped below $12,000, I played in smaller stakes games until I built my bankroll up again. Remember, I had to fund my poker from playing poker, not from an outside source.

You are not a professional. You are playing for fun and entertainment. And I hope your income from your other activities is more than your hourly win rate at poker. You need enough to play each session comfortably, without fear of going bust. You may choose to keep a separate poker bankroll, which I recommend, but you don't have to. When you want to play, you can draw it from other funds. I urge you to keep records. If you cannot beat the game and find that over time you have lost over $3,000 playing say $3–$6 poker, stop and reevaluate your game. The players who delude themselves lose year after year because they are often afraid to work out just how much they lose.

"Okay, Okay. So how much for each session?" you ask impatiently. Well, in a $3–$6 **structured** game you will need $72 (12 big bets, if there is a three-raise limit rule) to cover a hand in which the betting is capped in each betting round. Very rare indeed. So you should buy into a $3–$6 game for at least $80. In fact, I would say that in a $3–$6 game you should buy in for $200 and have another $400 in your pocket. If you blow through this in a single session, you should probably stop and reassess. You may be very unlucky but are more probably being outplayed.

This book is meant to enable you to play games up to $10–$20. So follow the preceding ratios, which are guidelines to what you should bring to the table. In a $6–$12 game, I would buy in for $400 and have another $800 available. In a $5–$10, buy in for $300 and have another $600 available. These are only guidelines, but if you play as suggested, in passive games, you will hardly ever need to go to your pocket.

Now you could take $600 and play in a $15–$30 game. You may get lucky and book a win, but you will feel very uncomfortable, since each betting round is draining so much of your stake. This is a type of adrenaline rush some people enjoy. I strongly advise against this. Instead, play at a moderate level with a big bankroll, and this way you can enjoy yourself for many hours at the table, without the constant fear of busting out. This will mean that you will make better playing decisions and have a less stressful time. Hell, if you wanted stress you could be at work, right? Play within your means if you want to have fun.

Unusual Game Formats

POT-LIMIT AND NO-LIMIT

Big bet poker. You have seen it on TV. It is thrilling and nerve racking. Should you play it for cash? No. At least not yet. I enjoy pot-limit and no-limit poker and so do many good players, but to a beginner, these games are minefields. The skills needed are beyond the scope of this book, but limit play will be an excellent foundation if you wish to move on to pot-limit and no-limit poker. Does this mean that the top pot-limit players and no-limit players are more skilled than the top limit players? Not at all. But different skills are demanded, and as a beginner you could lose your playing bankroll very fast in a pot-limit or no-limit game. Avoid them for now.

SPREAD-LIMIT GAMES

In **spread-limit** games, you can, instead of betting a fixed amount on each betting round, bet a range on the first two and last two rounds of betting. For example, if the limit is described as $1–$4–$8–$8, it means that on the first two betting rounds you can bet a minimum of $1 and a maximum of $4 and on the last two rounds you can bet a minimum of $1 and a maximum of $8.

Everything that has been said already can be applied here. However, if you come in for a raise, Pre-Flop, you should usually bet the maximum, thus effectively charging the weaker hands top dollar to continue and maximize their mistakes. If you are not betting, but say drawing to a flush or straight, check and hope your opponents let you in cheaply for less than the maximum bet or raise. In effect you are getting much better odds and implied odds for your draw, and this is again a mistake made by your opponents that makes you money. Now if you make your straight or flush draw, bet the maximum. Actually, you are playing a crippled form of no-limit poker in which you punish opponents for drawing against the odds and punish them for not betting strongly enough when they have the best hand. As long as you believe you have the best hand, bet the maximum and draw only when you have the odds. In spread limit, this may mean that against poor players you get the opportunity to play many more drawing hands because you are getting the correct odds more frequently.

If you start Pre-Flop with a mediocre or drawing hand and call for the minimum, fold if someone bets the maximum at you, especially if the hand does not play well in a shorthanded pot. You probably do not have the best hand, and the implied odds have all but disappeared. Calling in these situations will be a certain chip drainer.

Mostly unusual formats are just that—unusual. If a format is unfamiliar and you are uncomfortable, don't play. This book deals with the most common scenarios and one that you should find in most casinos. As you can see, you can sit down at a poker table with a moderate bankroll, and if you play as I suggest, you will be able to play for a few hours with very little risk of going bust. You could also win a tidy sum too! Essentially I am teaching you how to have fun at the casino, and that is the name of the game for the casual player, but I am also suggesting that it is more fun to play a disciplined, winning game with sufficient cash, than a loose, reckless, or wild game. The fun becomes not only in beating the opposition but in the constant resolution and mental challenge to make the best decisions possible and to strive to improve your skills constantly.

CHAPTER TWELVE

Moving Up to Bigger Games and Further Study

IF YOU HAVE read, studied, and practiced everything in the preceding chapters, you are already a far better player than the vast majority of low-limit players you will meet. In fact, if you keep practicing and studying this book, you will quickly dominate the games and become a consistent winner. When you reach this point, you may have the desire to move up to bigger games. To do so and be a winner there, against better players, you will need to develop some skills and familiarize yourself with concepts beyond the scope of this book. Everything you have learned here will form an excellent foundation, as you now have the fundamental concepts and attitudes necessary to play winning poker.

I stress that you can have a lot of fun, at low risk, and make some nice money at the lower limits. The higher limits are not necessarily more fun or always more lucrative, so there is no rush to go to those games. When you feel you are ready, here are a list of books that will help you. I will describe the ones that I believe are a "must read" for anyone who wishes to become a more skilled player. Finally, if you become really skilled, or even a world champion, then good for you, but I hope never to meet you at the table!

Must-Reads

Hold 'em Poker for Advanced Players (21st Century Edition)
by David Sklansky and Mason Malmuth
(1999, Henderson, NV: Two Plus Two Publishing)

It would be fair to describe this book as the essential manual for the limit game. All players of my generation owe an enormous debt to these two authors for their analysis of the game and their promulgation and elucidation of key concepts. This is a book that you should become deeply familiar with before moving up to bigger games. Any book or essay by either of these poker authorities is worth reading. They have tremendous insights and prodigious analytical abilities.

The Theory of Poker
by David Sklansky
(1989, Henderson, NV: Two Plus Two Publishing)

If you have not read this book, you are doing yourself a great disservice. It is truly a seminal work that should be on every serious poker player's bookshelf and read many times. David Sklansky gives an exhaustive analysis of key concepts that will deepen your understanding of all forms of poker. Many people regard this as the best book ever written on poker, and I would agree with them.

Gambling Theory and Other Topics
by Mason Malmuth
(1990, Henderson, NV: Two Plus Two Publishing)

Mason Malmuth deals with a number of important gambling theories such as nonself-weighting gambling strategies. He offers advice on such topics as bankroll requirements and tournaments. Anything written by Malmuth on poker is worth reading.

Books You Should Read

Super/System 2: A Course in Power Poker
Doyle Brunson and others
(2005, New York: Cardoza Publishing)

Many people consider the original edition of this book, *Doyle Brunson's Super System* (Cardoza, 1979),.to be a near poker bible. It certainly has governed the style of no-limit Hold'em play for a generation. *Super/System 2* is a heavily revised second edition and companion volume, and is really a series of extended essays on different poker forms written by leading poker players. Apart from Hold'em, the authors discuss 7-Card Stud, Omaha (high forms and split forms) and the exotic game of Triple Draw. The book covers limit, pot-limit, and no-limit poker. It also has an extensive "tips" section from Mike Caro. This book gives a very well rounded view of poker. My only criticism is that it tries to cover too much and therefore ends up not saying enough about each game! To play well in any of the games it mentions, you need more extensive instruction than what is offered in this volume: You will need other books that deal exclusively with your chosen poker game, be it Stud, Hold'em, or Omaha. Also, it assumes that readers will be playing in bigger games than most people actually play in. That aside, Brunson selects top players to author these essays, and they all have very valuable things to say about poker strategy and tactics, which is especially useful for more advances players. It remains one of the best books on poker and repays careful study.

The Complete Book of Hold'em Poker
by Gary Carson
(2001, New York: Lyle Stuart/Citadel Press)

This book has many valuable discussions and alternative views on poker theory. It is dense with information and touches on a very large range of topics including poker maths, tournaments, turning pro, and player types.

Worth a Read

Caro's Book of Poker Tells, also called *The Body Language of Poker*
by Mike Caro
(2003, New York: Cardoza)

Mike Caro is the best-known authority on poker tells, the unconscious actions many make that give away their real intentions. Caro was the first player to describe these, and the book is valuable. New books on the same topic worth reading are:

Beyond Tells: Power Poker Psychology
by James A. McKenna, Ph.D.
(2005, New York: Lyle Stuart/Citadel Press)

Inside the Poker Mind
by John Feeney, Ph.D.
(2000, Henderson, NV: Two Plus Two Publishing)

John Feeney deals with a number of key poker skills and emotional as well as conceptual elements of poker. Many interesting topics are discussed intelligently.

The Psychology of Poker
by Alan N. Schoonmaker, Ph.D.
(2000, Henderson, NV: Two Plus Two Publishing)

Alan is a great guy, and he has written the most extensive book on poker psychology currently available. As well as having a Ph.D. in psychology, Alan is also a keen player. Many valuable insights pepper this volume. Personally, I do not wholly buy into everything he has to say about the personality classification of individuals, but despite this, a lot of what he says makes sense.

Middle Limit Holdem Poker
by Bob Ciaffone and Jim Brier
(2002, Las Vegas, NV: Bob Ciaffone)

Ciaffone is a top professional cash and tournament player and author. Brier is also a professional and author. This book is full of exhaustive analysis of different hands and situations and will certainly help you improve your poker thinking.

Winning Low-Limit Hold'em
by Lee Jones
(2000, Pittsburgh, PA: ConJelCo)

Lee Jones covers much the same ground as my book, but you should still read it. This book helped me more when I was starting out than any other single volume, and I still benefit from reading it. You will too.

Small Stakes Hold 'em
by Edward Miller, David Sklansky, and Mason Malmuth
(2004, Henderson, NV: Two Plus Two)

An advanced book on making money in the low-limit game. Like all books from these authors, it offers solid information. Unlike other books from these authors, it examines the low-limit game and shows how this game is essentially different from the higher limits and what skills you need to win money consistently.

This is a personal selection of books that I have found particularly helpful and that I believe offer solid advice. It is not an exhaustive review of poker titles, and many good, new books are coming out in the next couple of years. However, if you read these books, study them, and apply them, you will have given yourself a very well rounded poker education, and you will be well on your way to becoming a very good player. In addition, there are a number of poker discussion groups on the Internet that offer lively discussions on the game. They are easy to find if you look for them using search engines.

Glossary of Poker Terms, Phrases, and Jargon

In this glossary, you will find almost every term you will run across in a Hold'em game. I have expanded on some of these on my website at www.holdempokernow.com. Check it out, as you will also find supplementary articles and links to poker and gaming.

AA (Two Aces) Many poker hands have nicknames. This is the best Pre-Flop hand you can have in Hold'em. It is sometimes called "American Airlines," "Pocket Rockets," or "Bullets."

Action (The Action) This is the betting in a specific hand or game. If the dealer says, "The action is on you," it means that it is your turn to act. A game with a lot of betting and raising is said to have lots of action.

Active Player Any player still in the pot.

Add-On In poker tournaments there is often one final opportunity to re-buy a specific number of tournament chips. This is the add-on.

Advertise Showing down a mediocre hand with the deliberate intention of posing as a weak, loose player and establishing an image, perhaps false, as such.

Aggressive A style of play where the player bets, raises, and re-raises a lot. Some people think all good players are aggressive. Not so. They are *selectively* aggressive.

All-In   When a player has all of his chips in the pot he is said to be all-in. In table-stakes games, this can only be the amount of money you actually have on the table at the start of the hand. Once a player is all-in, he cannot call additional bets or raises. Any additional bets go into a separate side pot in which the all-in player has no stake.

Angle   A legal but ethically dubious practice. (This definition may apply to the vast majority of U.S. lawyers come to think of it.) For example, if you pretend to go to your chips out of turn to discourage a player from betting.

Ante   Found in some poker games such as Seven-Card Stud or Draw Poker, there is a small forced bet at the beginning of each round of play that every player has to put into the pot. The purpose is to encourage people to play and not just wait for the best hand, which would be the best play if no ante were required. There is no ante in Hold'em, but there are two forced bets called the "Big Blind" and the "Small Blind," which every player has to put into the pot when he is one or two to the left of the dealer button.

Backdoor   Catching the Turn and River card to make a drawing hand. A "backdoor flush draw" is made when you hold only one card of the suit that you need and it appears on the Flop. If two more of the same suit come on the Turn and River, you have made a backdoor flush, also known as making a runner-runner hand.

Bad Beat   If a player holds a hand that is a heavy favorite to win and a hand that is a heavy underdog beats it, the losing player is said to have taken a bad beat. If you sit around a poker table long enough, some players are likely to regale you with stories of the bad beats they have taken. Everybody takes bad beats, and the better you play the more you are going to take. Hearing about them becomes tedious. If I suspect a fellow player is about to start whining about a bad beat, I stop him and tell him that I charge $5 to listen to a bad beat story. This usually ensures that you do not become a bad beat misery aunt at the table!

Bad Beat Jackpot   See Jackpot.

Bad Game   A game in which your opponents outclass you and are too good for you to expect a win. You should avoid games in which you are the underdog, as you will invariably lose your money to better players.

Bankroll   The total amount of money you have available to wager. This is usually and should be substantially more than what you bring to the table for an individual session of play.

Belly Buster   An inside straight draw. When you hit a belly buster, it means you drew the card to make your inside straight. A double belly buster is a hand that is composed of two inside straight draws, giving you the same odds as an open-ended straight draw.

Best of It   A situation in which a wager can be expected to be profitable over time. In a table game such as roulette, the casino or house is said always to have the best of it because the odds are always in favor of the house.

Bet (or "Bet Out")   To put money into the pot that other players must match to remain in the hand.

Bet for Value   To bet in order to be called by an inferior hand. You are betting in the hope that your opponents will call but not fold, so you can make more money.

Betting Round   The series of checks, bets, or raises made in turn by all eligible players before more cards are dealt or there is a showdown. In Hold'em there is a maximum of four betting rounds in each hand.

Bettor   The player who first puts chips into the pot in any given round.

Big Blind   The larger of the two blinds in a Hold'em game. The Big Blind is usually a sum equal to the full first round bet, although in some pot-limit and no-limit games, it may be less. The Big Blind is the player two seats to the left of the dealer button. Each player becomes big blind in turn as the dealer button moves clockwise around the table.

Big Slick Slang for ace and king, before the Flop.

Blank A card that is of no apparent value to any player's hand and does not affect the standing of the players in the pot.

Blind The forced bets that players must make to begin a betting round. In most limit Hold'em games there are two blinds: the Big Blind and the Small Blind. The Big Blind is usually one full bet, and the Small Blind is half or occasionally one third or two thirds of the Big Blind. The player whose turn it is to put up this bet is said to be "in the blind."

Bluff To bet or raise with a hand that you do not believe to be the best hand and has little or no chance of becoming so, even when there are more cards to come. This is a pure bluff. You can only win if all the other players remaining in the pot fold. You should bluff infrequently in low-limit games and just about never against a very poor player. Very poor players will tend to call, making bluffing an unprofitable play against them.

Board All the community cards in a Hold'em game are said to make up the board. They are placed face up in the middle of the table, and any player can use these cards to make up his hand.

Boat Slang for a full house.

Bottom Pair Pairing the lowest card on the board.

Broadway An ace-high straight.

Brush The casino staff member responsible for seating players in a game. He "brushes them in." He ensures that games are filled in an orderly fashion and maintains a waiting list if the games are full.

Burn (or Burn Card) To burn a card means to discard the top card from the deck face down. The dealer will burn a card before each betting round and before he puts down the next community card on the board. The purpose is to provide a security measure to prevent players from gaining an advantage by catching a glimpse of the next card.

Bust To lose all of one's playing stake.

Busted Hand A hand that does not develop into anything of value. A flush draw that never actually becomes a flush is said to be a "busted flush."

Button A white disk placed in front of a player who indicates that player is the nominal dealer. The player "on the button" is the last player to act in each betting round except the first. The live player closest to the button will act last in each betting round. For example, when another player says, "The button re-raised," he means the player on the button re-raised.

Buy ("... the Pot" or "... Button") To buy the pot is to bluff hoping to win the pot when nobody calls. A player is said to buy the button when he is not on the button but bets or raises hoping to make other players between him and the button fold and thus ensuring that he is last to act on each subsequent betting round.

Buy-In The minimum stake required to sit in a particular game.

Call To put into the pot a sum of money equal to the last bet or raise.

Call a Raise Cold To call a double bet, that is, a bet and a raise.

Caller Player who calls.

Calling Station A passive player who calls a lot but rarely bets or raises. Many players like this usually make for a profitable, low-risk game.

Cap To put in the last permitted raise in a betting round. The player who does this is said to have "capped the pot." When a player says "cap it," he is announcing that he is making the last permitted raise in that round of betting. Most card rooms allow a maximum of three raises in each betting round. If there are only two players contesting a pot, it is said to be heads up, and then an unlimited number of raises are usually allowed. Some players like to say "cappuccino"—very yuppie.

Cards Speak Rule This means that the best hand at the showdown will win the pot. You do not need to declare your hand. The dealer will let the cards speak and give the pot to the player with the best hand.

Case The last card of a specific rank in the deck is said to be the case card.

Center Pot Alternative name for the main pot that is formed in the center of the table as the dealer collects chips from each betting round.

Chase When a player continues in a hand (with a draw), with a hand that he knows is inferior to his opponent's hand, he is said to be chasing. In low-limit games, players often chase with very poor hands.

Check To not bet with the option to call or raise later in the betting round. If everybody checks, then the next betting round is started.

Check-Raise To check and then raise after an opponent bets. Some players maintain that check-raising is unethical. Utter hogwash. Check-raising is a vital tactic in Limit Hold'em, and you should never play in a card room that does not allow it. Without it, the players on the button and in late position have an enormous edge.

Chips The tokens used in place of money in a game. Some people also call these "checks." Also, the snacks brought to you (in the United States at least) by seductive waitstaff during a game.

Cinch The best possible hand given the board when all the cards are out. Also called "the nuts."

Come Hand A drawing hand.

Community Cards   The cards dealt face up in the center of the board that active players use to form their hands. Hold'em is described as a community card style of poker.

Complete Hand   A hand that is defined by all five cards. It can be a straight, flush, full house, four of a kind, or a straight flush.

Connector   A starting hand in Hold'em in which the two cards are one rank apart, for example, 89 or QJ. Suited connectors are when both cards are of the same suit.

Counterfeit   To pretend to be a good player: not really, that was a bad joke. When a board card duplicates one of your pocket cards and makes your hand less valuable, you have been "counterfeited." For example, you hold 8 10 and the board is 79J on the Flop, if a 10 comes on the Turn, your hand now has just about no value. The 10 counterfeited you.

Crack   When a hand, usually a big hand like pocket aces or kings get beaten, it is said to be cracked.

Cripple-the-Deck   This means that you hold most or all the cards that somebody would want to have to make their hand. When you Flop four of a kind you cripple the deck. When you cripple the deck, you will probably win your hand, but you may not get much action.

Crying Call   A call with a hand, usually at the end, that you think has a small chance of winning.

Cut the Pot   To take a percentage from each pot. Also called the "rake." This is how the casino makes money from a poker game.

Dead Hand   A hand that cannot continue to play because of an irregularity. A player's hand is declared dead if he is not at the table when the action is on him.

Dead Man's Hand   Aces and eights, so-called because this is the hand that Wild Bill Hickok was holding when he was shot at a poker table in Deadwood, North Dakota.

Dead Money   Money in the pot that has been put there by players who have already folded their hand.

Deuce   The two card.

Dog   Shortened form of "underdog."

Dominated Hands   A hand that will usually lose to a better hand that people commonly play. For example A5 is dominated by AQ. Consistently playing dominated hands is a certain way to lose money.

Draw   A hand that is not yet a good hand but may become one if the right cards fall. You may be drawing to a straight or a flush.

Drawing Dead   Drawing to a hand that even when made will not win the pot. If you are drawing to a straight when your opponent has a flush, for example, you are said to be drawing dead.

Draw Out   To make a drawing hand to beat an opponent who was beating you before the draw. You have "drawn out" on the other player.

Double Belly Buster   See Belly Buster.

Doyle (Texas Dolly) Brunson (the man and the hand)   A poker legend, author of a book many consider poker's bible, and two-time winner of the *World Series of Poker*. The hand 10 2 is also called a "Doyle Brunson" because Doyle won successive world championships holding this hand. Whenever you see it, do what I am certain Doyle does with it 99 percent of the time: muck it without a second thought. It is a true garbage hand.

Early Position   The next three seats after the big blind.

Effective Odds   The ratio between what you expect to win, if you make your hand, and the sum total of the bets you will have to call from the present round of betting to the end of the hand. (See chapter 3 for more information about odds.)

Equity This is a somewhat controversial term. Some poker theorists use this term to refer to the value of a particular hand or combination of cards. More commonly it refers to your "share" of the pot in relation to how much is in the pot and your chances of winning it. So if there is $120 in the pot and you have a 50 percent chance of winning, it could be said to have $60 equity in the pot. I personally question the value of such a term, as you will go on to win the pot or win nothing. For myself, I believe that this notion of pot equity causes players to make questionable decisions.

Expectation Over the long run, every hand can be said to have a positive or negative expectation, which is the average profit or loss it will show over time. Ideally, one should never play hands that have an overall negative expectation. Of course, in the short run, even the worst hand can win a pot if the board cards favor it. Expectation also refers to the overall win rate if you make a certain play. For example, you may bluff three times and fail twice, but if the one time your bluff succeeds, you win more than the combined total of your three bets—your play has a positive expectation. Win rate can also be expressed as an expectation, which is the average hourly rate you expect to win over the long haul. The actual wins and losses in a single session can fluctuate widely, however.

Extra Blinds When a new player enters a game, he usually has to put up an amount equal to the big blind. He "posts" a blind, and this is sometimes called an "extra blind." There may be more than one extra blind if more than one new player enters the game.

Family Pot If all or almost all the players call before the Flop, this is called a "family pot."

Fast Yes, I know you know what fast means, but in poker to play fast does not mean to play quickly! It means to play a hand aggressively, usually betting and raising as much as possible. You typically play fast when you have a good but not unbeatable hand and you do not wish to give drawing hands a chance to catch up.

Favorite   The hand that has the best chance of winning before all the cards are dealt.

Fifth Street   An alternative name for the last community card or River card in Hold'em. Stud players sometimes use this term.

Fill   To draw a card to make a hand. If the board pairs, to make your set a full house. Your hand has been "filled up."

Fish   A weak, aimless player.

Flat Call   To call a bet without raising.

Flop   The first three simultaneously dealt, exposed, community cards. Flop is also used as a verb, for example, "I flopped two pair."

Flush   Five cards of the same suit.

Fold   To drop out of a hand and not call a bet or raise.

Four Flush   Four cards to a flush

Four of a Kind   Four cards of the same rank.

Fourth Street   An alternative name for the Turn card.

Free Card   A Turn or River card that you get without having to call a bet. Sometimes a raise on the Flop is made in the hope that every player checks to you on the next round and thus gives you a free card. This is especially valuable if you are drawing to a hand.

Free Roll   A situation where two players have the same hand, but one has a chance to make a better hand. For example, two players both hold a pair of aces before the Flop. If the Flop comes down with three suited cards, the player holding the ace of that suit will be said to have a free roll on his opponent. He cannot lose the hand, but if another card of the same suit appears on the Turn or River, he can win the whole pot. Sometimes casinos offer free tournaments as a promotion, and these are sometimes called "free roll tournaments."

Full House Three cards of one rank and two of another. Three aces and two kings would be called "aces over kings."

Gutshot A draw to an inside straight. Also called a "belly buster."

Heads Up To play against a single opponent. Some players specialize in this type of play, but most low-limit players have no clue how to play heads up. Avoid it until you are much better. You can lose a lot faster if you do not know what you are doing and even if you do!

Hit When the Flop hits you, it contains cards that help your hand.

Hourly Rate The amount of money a player expects to win on average. This average rate comes in big fits and starts. It is easily possible to win or lose forty times your hourly rate in a single session, even if overall you are a winning player.

House The casino or card room that runs the game. The house makes its money by collecting a time charge or by taking a small sum, or rake, from each pot.

Implied Odds Pot odds that do not currently exist, but may be included in your calculation based on bets you expect to win if you make your hand. It is this consideration that sometimes allows you to make a call, even though strictly speaking the pot is not offering you the proper odds. (See chapter 3 for more details.)

Inside Straight A straight that can only be made with a card of one rank. For example, if you had an ace and king and the Flop was 9 10 J, only a queen could give you a straight.

Jackpot One of the rare instances in poker in which losing is better than winning! A jackpot is a form of special promotion now offered widely by casinos and card rooms in which a special bonus is paid to a player whose very good hand is beaten by an even better hand. This is sometimes called a "bad beat jackpot." Jackpots can be over $100,000 in large and online casinos. They are funded by the house taking a small rake from each pot. While jackpots may encourage some players to enter the game, many have criticized them. First, because they lower the amount one can win from a pot but also because jackpot money is often lost to the game forever. This is because when players win single large sums, they are more likely to use it to pay bills, mortgages, buy houses, vacations, cars, or boats and not put it back in the game. This means that there is less money around for winning players to win. However, jackpots are good for realtors, car and boat dealers, and credit card companies.

Kicker An unpaired card used to determine the better hand of two equally ranked hands. For example, if when all the cards are dealt, the top hand is a pair of aces. A player holding AK will win over a player having AQ, assuming that the pair of aces is the best hand. The player with the AQ has been "out kicked" by the player holding the king.

Late Position A position in the round of betting in which you act after most of the other players. Usually the button and one to the right of the button.

Legitimate Hand A hand with true value, not a bluffing hand.

Limit The predetermined amount that a player may bet on any round of betting.

Limp In When a player calls rather than raises on the first round of betting, he is said to have limped in.

Live One A bad, loose player who loses a lot of money.

Lock A lock is a hand guaranteed to win at least part of the pot. (See also Nuts).

Loose Playing loose simply means playing more hands than optimum and holding on to them for a longer time. A loose table is a table with many loose players. Most low-limit players are loose players. Loose isn't always bad—excessively tight play can be equally costly, especially at high levels of play. A loose call is borderline, inadvisable, or even incorrect. *He was playing so loose, it seemed like he was playing every hand he was dealt.*

Main pot When a player goes all-in, in a table-stakes game, that player is only eligible to win the main pot—the pot consisting of those bets he was able to match. Additional bets are then placed in a side pot by the dealers and are contested among the remaining players.

Make To make a hand means to get a decent hand that has a shot at winning the pot.

Maniac A maniac is a player who plays extremely loosely and aggressively, often betting, raising, and re-raising with poor cards in poor situations. Maniacs at the table tend to increase the fluctuations in your bankroll considerably. Please see chapter 10 for what to do when a maniac is at the table.

Middle Pair If there are three cards of different ranks on the Flop and you pair the middle one, you have middle pair.

Middle Position The fourth, fifth and sixth seats to the left of the big blind.

Miss When the Flop contains no cards that help your hand.

Monster An extremely strong hand, one that is almost certain to win the pot.

Muck The pile of discarded cards in front of the dealer or the act of putting cards in this pile, therefore taking them out of play. The common house rule is that as soon as the cards touch the muck, they are ineligible to win the pot.

No-Limit As you might guess, any game in which there is no limit on the sizes of bets and raises. All the major tournaments have a no-limit Hold'em game as their premier game. The *World Series of Poker* is a no-limit Hold'em tournament. Note that in table-stakes games, players are still limited to the amount of money they have in front of them.

Nuts (or Nut-) The nuts is the best possible hand. In Hold'em, the nuts can never be less than trips. "Nut xxx" is sometimes used to refer to the best hand of a particular type, especially a straight or flush. You must quickly learn to recognize what the nuts is for any given board in Hold'em.

Odds A ratio of two probabilities, usually the probability of making a hand to the probability of not making the hand. Thus if you have a 25 percent chance of making a hand, the odds are 3 to 1 against your making it. In poker, this is especially important in considering pot odds.

Off-Suit Not of the same suit. Sometimes abbreviated to just "off." "I'll play K10 off-suit occasionally, but only in late position if there has been no raise."

One-Gap See Inside Straight.

Open To open, or open betting, is to make the first bet in a betting round. For example: *I opened with a small pair in late position hoping to make a set on the Flop.*

Open-Ender See Open-Ended Straight Draw.

Open-Ended Straight (Draw) A straight draw is open-ended if it consists of four consecutive cards (none of them an ace). The straight can be completed at either end. (See also Double Belly Buster and Inside Straight.)

Option When a player posts a live blind, as they first sit down or after they have been away from the table for a long time, that player is given the option to raise when the action is on them even if no one else has raised. The dealer will typically say something like "your option," to remind them.

Out An out is a card that will improve your hand, usually one that you think will make it a winner. In Hold'em, an open-ended straight draw has eight outs (the four cards of each rank will complete the straight). But it may be only six outs if there are two suited cards on the table and someone else is drawing for the flush.

Outdraw To make a better hand than an opponent does by merit of the cards you draw.

Over Button In some games, players can take "over" buttons, which means they are willing to play at higher limits. Anytime everyone left in the hand has an over button, the limits go up.

Overcall Any additional call after a bet is first called. Player A bets, player B calls, player C overcalls.

Overcard A card higher than the highest card on the board. If you hold KJ and the Flop is J95, you have top pair with an overcard. If the Flop is 10 9 2, you just have two overcards.

Overpair A pocket pair higher than the highest card on the board. If you hold KK and the Flop is Q5, you have an overpair.

Paint A jack, king, or queen (a card with a painted picture on it).

Pair Two cards of the same rank. If you hold AA, you have a pair.

Pass To fold.

Passive Passive is a style of play that is characterized by reluctance to bet and raise. This does not mean tight play. A typical loose-passive player will call with almost anything, but raise only with very powerful hands (see Calling Station). A passive table is one with many passive players, so that, for example, few hands are raised before the Flop.

Pay Off To call a bet by a player you're reasonably sure has you beaten. Weak players pay you off more often than strong players. This makes for a profitable game.

Perfect When you only have one way to make a hand. If you hold 9J you need three perfect cards, 8 10 Q, for the nut straight. To "catch perfect" is to hit perfect cards.

Play To play a hand in poker means to make it past the first round of betting. In Hold'em this means calling the big blind. If some-one says they haven't played a hand in hours, they are complain-ing that they haven't had cards good enough to play. To make a play, or put a play on (someone), means to present a pattern of behavior inconsistent with your cards that will mislead your opponents and cause them to make a mistake. This could mean bluffing them out of a pot, but it can also mean getting them to call when you have a strong hand, or more generally, anything (legitimate) intended to manipulate their behavior, in order to cause them to make errors.

Play Back (at) To play back at someone is to raise their opening bet or to re-raise their raise.

Play the Board In Hold'em if your best five-card hand uses the five community cards, you are said to be playing the board. The best you can do in this situation is to split the pot with anyone who calls. If you are sure the board cannot be improved, you should bet, as very poor players who misread the board may fold.

Pocket The two cards dealt to you face down or the first two face down are called your "pocket cards."

Pocket Pair Two pocket cards of the same rank.

Poker Poker refers to a number of card games. This book is about the most popular form, Texas Hold'em. A majority of poker games do share some common features, especially betting in rounds and the ranking of hands. The varieties played in home games proba-bly number in the thousands. Some common public card room games include Texas Hold'em, Seven-Card Stud, and Omaha.

Position Position refers to your place at the table, in relation to the nominal dealer, and defines the order of betting within a particular betting round. The first few players to act are said to be in early position, the next few in middle position, and the last few in late position. Late position is best, since you have the advantage of knowing what your opponents have done. You can play more hands from later positions. In Hold'em, position is fixed from one round of betting to the next, and the dealer, the player on the button, is always in last position and is last to act in all but the first round of betting when the big blind acts first. More generally, to have position on someone is to be in a position to bet after them, either during a particular hand or in general. You have position on anyone sitting immediately to your right, since you will usually be able to act after him.

Position Bet   A position bet is a bet made more on the strength of one's position than solely on the strength of one's hand. A player on the button in Hold'em is in good position to "steal" the blinds if no one else opens the betting.

Post   To post a bet is to place your chips in the pot (or, commonly, out in front of you so that your bet can be counted). In poker, posting usually means a forced bet, such as posting the big blind, usually equivalent to one full first-round bet.

Pot   All the money in the middle of the poker table that goes to the winner of the hand is called the "pot." Any player who has not yet folded his hand is said to be "in the pot." A player who has called an initial bet is said to have entered the pot.

Pot Limit   Any game in which the maximum bet or raise is the size of the pot. For raises, the size of the pot includes the call, so if the pot is $100 and player A bets $100, player B can bet a total of $400 for a maximum raise; calling the $100 and then raising the size of the $300 pot.

Pot Odds   The ratio of the amount of money in the pot to the amount of money it will cost you to call a bet. The greater the pot odds, the more likely you should be to call because you will have to win fewer times over the long haul to make that a positive expectation.

Presto   A nickname for pocket 5's. This nickname comes from the Internet newsgroup rec.gambling.poker (www.recpoker.com) and is sometimes used among the readership of that newsgroup to identify other members.

Prop   Short for proposition player. (See Proposition Player.)

Proposition Player   A proposition player, or prop, is a player who is paid by the house (casino) to play poker, usually in order to keep games going or to get games started. Props are paid a salary, but they gamble with their own money. Props either learn how to play pretty solid poker or run out of money. (See also Shill.)

Protect   To protect a hand (usually a made hand) is to bet in order to lessen the chances of anyone outdrawing you, the bet inducing them to fold an inferior hand or a drawing hand. A hand that needs protection is one that is almost certainly best right now but that is vulnerable to being outdrawn. Large pots make it difficult to protect hands, especially in limit poker where the bet size is predetermined, since players will be willing to chase more long shots, as the pot is often offering them the correct odds or close to the correct odds. The structure of a game has a large impact on how easy it is to protect a hand, as do the personalities of the players at the table. It's easiest to protect a hand in no-limit Hold'em play where you can make it as expensive as your chip stack allows for someone to draw to a hand. To protect your cards is also to place a chip or some other small object (such objects vary widely from the quaint to the downright bizarre) on top of them so that they aren't accidentally mucked by the dealer, mixed with another player's discarded cards, or otherwise become dead.

Provider   A provider is a poker player who makes the game profitable for the other players at the table. Similar in meaning to fish (no, not the type in your local aquarium, but the aimless players found in some games), although the provider has a somewhat less negative connotation. A provider might be a decent player who just happens to be playing out of his league. He provides for the better players, probably something he does not really intend to do!

Push What the dealer does with the pot when he figures out who the winner is. He pushes it to the winner!

Put On To put someone on a hand is to guess what he is holding.

Quads Four of a Kind.

Rabbit Hunting Rabbit hunting is the act of asking to see what cards would have come up if a hand had continued. It also means rifling through the muck and is usually illegal in most card rooms.

Rack Most usually the plastic racks that hold 100 chips in 5 stacks of 20. If someone asks for a rack, it usually means they're about to leave the table. Someone is said to be "racking up" a game if he is winning a lot of money at the table. In most card rooms you cannot place chips in a rack on the table. In one card room I played in where this rule was not in force, an attractive woman was doing well and had placed about $1,000 worth of chips in two racks on the table. One new, slightly inebriated player on joining the game stared at the chips and then blurted out, in admiration, "Nice rack!" She was not amused, but I still believe he meant the chips.

Rag A card, usually a low card, that, when it appears, has no apparent effect on the hand. A Flop of 963 is a rag Flop—few playable hands match the Flop well. If the table shows KQJ10, all diamonds, a deuce of hearts on the River is a rag.

Rail The rail is the sideline at a poker table separating spectators from the field of play. Watching from the rail means watching a poker game as a spectator. People on the rail are sometimes called "railbirds."

Railbird Someone watching a game from the rail.

Rainbow Three cards of different suits, usually on the Flop.

Raise After someone has opened the betting in a round, a player can increase, or raise, the amount of the bet. For example, if the betting limit is $5 and player A bets $5, player B can fold, call the $5, or raise it to $10.

Rake The money removed from each pot by the house. Medium- and higher-limit games typically have a time charge rather than a rake. A typical Atlantic City low-limit rake is 10 percent of the pot up to a $4 maximum. An excessive rake can make a game unprofitable, even for good players. Generally speaking, one must play a shade tighter in pot-raked games.

Rank Each card has a suit and a rank. The ten of diamonds and the ten of spades have the same rank. A pair is two cards of the same rank.

Read To read someone is to have a good idea from their play (or through tells) what their cards may be. To have a read on someone is to have a good understanding of how he plays.

Redraw A way to improve your hand further after hitting a draw is a redraw. For example, if you hold 10♦, 9♦, and the Flop is J♦, Q♦, 3♣, you have a flush draw. If the Turn is the ace of diamonds, you have made your flush and picked up an inside straight-flush redraw.

Represent To bet or raise in such a way as to indicate that you have a certain hand. For instance, when you bet or raise after the third suited card hits the board, you are representing a flush, even if you don't actually have one.

Re-raise Any raise after the first raise in a round. Player A bets, player B raises, player C (or A) re-raises.

Ring Game Poker played for cash. The term "ring game" is used to differentiate such games from tournaments.

River The last of five of the five community cards that makes up the board. Sometimes called "fifth street."

Rock A player who plays extremely tight is a rock. Many retirees play like this. Rocks don't create a lot of action, but when they enter a pot, more often than not, they're in as a favorite. This is a winning strategy at some tables, especially at a table full of very loose players, but it makes them very predictable. Players with more varied strategies will generally beat them handily.

Rock Garden A table populated with rocks.

Rockets Or "pocket rockets"—a pair of aces Pre-Flop.

Round A round can refer to either a round of betting or a round of hands. A betting round usually begins after a card or several cards are dealt. Each player is given a chance to act, and the round ends when everyone has either folded or called the last bet or raise. Each round of betting is followed either by further dealing or by a showdown of cards. A round of hands consists of one hand dealt by each player at the table (or, when there is a house dealer, one hand with the dealer button at each position). In a round of Hold'em, you're in each position once.

Royal Straight Flush An ace-high straight flush is a royal straight flush or a royal flush or just a royal. It's the best hand in poker, played for high.

Runner-Runner A hand made on the last two cards. (See also Backdoor.)

Rush A player who wins a large number of pots in a short period is said to be on a rush. Some players feel superstitiously that a rush is an independent entity, and they will "play their rush" or "bet their rush" after winning a few pots—play looser and more aggressively or just be certain to play out each hand until the rush ends. Personally, I have always believed that the rush is a fallacy. Cards have no memory.

Sandbag Sandbagging usually means check-raising. Sandbagging sometimes means concealing your strength for the purpose of increasing your profit. Slowplaying is sometimes described as sandbagging. Check-raising or slowplaying, despite this derogatory nickname, are not unethical and are only considered such by the lamebrained.

Scare Card A card that when it appears makes a better hand more likely. In Hold'em, a third suited card on the River is a scare card because it makes a flush possible. Scare cards will often make it difficult for the best hand to bet and also offer a bluffing opportunity.

Seat Charge See Time Charge.

Seating List In most casino card rooms if there is no seat available for you when you arrive, you can put your name on a list to be seated when a seat becomes available. Typically, games are listed across the top of a board, and names are written below each game so that players are seated for games in the order in which they arrive.

Second Pair Same as middle pair. (See Middle Pair.)

See To call a bet is sometimes referred to as seeing it. Avoid saying this in casinos, despite what you may have seen in the movies. If you say, "I'll see you and raise," it will probably be called a "string bet." (See String Bet.)

Semi-bluff A bluff with a hand that is almost certainly second best now but may become the best hand if the right cards fall. The power of this play is that it can win three ways: by in fact being the best hand, by becoming the best hand, or by causing others to fold.

Set When you have a pocket pair and a third card of the same rank appears on the board, you have a set. (See Trips.)

Seven-Card Stud Of the poker games most commonly played in public card rooms, Seven-Card Stud is second only in popularity to Hold'em. In Seven-Card Stud (sometimes Seven Stud or just Stud), each player is dealt seven cards: two down, then four up, and a final card down. There is a round of betting after the first up card and after each subsequent card dealt. Stud is usually played with a small ante and a forced bet called a "bring in" on third street. In limit games, the bet size typically increases on fifth street.

Shill A shill is similar to a proposition player (see Proposition Play), except a shill gambles with the card room's money instead of his own.

Shootout A tournament format in which a single player ends up with the entire prize money or in which play continues at each table until only one player remains.

Short Stack A short stack is a stack that's too small to cover the likely betting in a hand. A player who has such a stack is said to be short stacked.

Shorthanded A game is said to be shorthanded when it falls below a certain number of players. In Hold'em, any game with five players or less is generally called "shorthanded." Since the number of players at a table has a significant impact on strategy, learning to play well shorthanded is an important skill. Avoid shorthanded play if you are a novice. It can be costly.

Showdown When all the betting is done, if more than one player is still in the pot, the showdown is the process of showing cards to determine who wins the pot. The last player to bet or raise is required to show his cards first, and any player can ask to see the hands of any callers at the showdown.

Show One Show All A common card room rule states that if a player shows his cards to anyone at the table, that player can be asked to show everyone else (even if the player would ordinarily not be required to show his hand). This usually comes up at the end of a hand that did not reach showdown. Obviously showing one's hand to someone else who has cards is illegal.

Shuffle Before each hand, the dealer mixes, or shuffles, the cards up in order to make their order as unpredictable as possible. Most casinos have fairly specific requirements for how the cards are to be shuffled.

Side Pot See Main Pot.

Slowplay To slowplay is to underbet a very strong hand. The purpose of slowplaying a hand is to give other players the chance to make stronger second-best hands and also to conceal the strength of your hand. Instead of betting early and risking the loss of future action, slowplay means checking and calling. It is of course best to slowplay when you have a hand that no one is likely to actually catch (for example, four of a kind). Most players slowplay far too much and then complain about getting outdrawn.

Slowroll To reveal one's hand slowly at showdown, often one card at a time, is to slowroll anyone else who thinks the pot might be his. This is usually only done with a winning hand, for the purpose of irritating other players. It is very bad poker manners, don't do it.

Small Blind The smaller of the two forced bets in Hold'em. The small blind is immediately to the left of the button and is first to act (in worst position) in all betting rounds except the Pre-Flop.

Smooth Call A type of slowplaying. To call one or more bets with a hand that would usually be raised with the intention of trapping players in later rounds.

Snap Off To beat someone, often a bluffer, and usually without an especially powerful hand is to snap them off.

Speed Speed refers to the level of aggression. Fast play is more aggressive, slow play (not slowplaying) is more passive. Good players may change speeds to disguise their play.

Speeding Someone who is caught bluffing is sometimes said to be caught speeding.

Splash (the pot)   To throw your chips into the pot, instead of placing them in front of you, is to splash the pot. Doing so annoys dealers, as it can make it difficult for the dealer to determine if you have bet the correct amount or to keep track of the action.

Split Pot   A hand in which two players showdown the same hand that results in a pot split between those two players.

Spread   When a card room starts a table for a particular game, it is said to spread that game.

Spread Limit   Betting limits in which there is a fixed minimum and maximum bet for each betting round, and any amount in between these limits may be bet. (See chapter 11 for more details.)

Stack   The amount of money you have in front of you on the poker table.

Steal   To (attempt to) steal a pot is to make a bet when it appears no one else has anything. Stealing blinds is often done from late position.

Steam   A steam raise is a raise made more out of frustration than out of strategic concerns. A player who is on tilt is sometimes said to be steaming. Steaming is a bad idea, but can be hard to avoid.

Straddle   The player immediately to the left of the small blind may raise before looking at his cards, effectively posting an additional blind bet. This is called a "straddle" or "live straddle." House rules often make these bets live so that the player who posts a live straddle has the option of raising when it's his turn again even if no one has re-raised. Straddling is a pretty dumb idea. Never do it.

Straight   A hand composed of five cards of consecutive ranks (aces count as high or low). The hand 23456 is a six-high straight, or a straight to the six. The hand 7 8 9 10 J is a jack-high straight, or a straight to the jack. In comparing straights, the straight to the higher card wins.

Straight Flush A hand consisting of five cards of consecutive ranks of the same suit. A straight flush is the strongest possible hand. Of two straight flushes, the one with the highest high card is better. An ace-high straight flush is often called a "royal flush" or a "royal straight flush" or just a "royal."

Street The cards that come out one at a time in a card game are sometimes referred to as different numbered streets. In Hold'em, players sometimes refer to the Turn and River as fourth and fifth street.

String Bet Most casinos require you to make your entire bet at once. In other words, you can't raise by putting out enough to call and then reach back to your stack for your raise. As well, since verbal statements are considered binding at most poker games, if you say, "I call your bet and raise you ten more," you have called, since the raise was added afterward. To be on the safe side, when you want to raise, it's best to say "raise" so that your bet won't be mistaken. The reason for the string bet rule is to prevent players from unfairly misleading other players about the size of their bet. By the way, when it comes to betting, the movies mostly have it wrong.

Structure The structure of a game refers to the details about the betting, blinds, and what may be bet on any round. In card rooms, games are typically posted along with shorthand for the limits. For example, $5–$10 Hold'em is usually a fixed-limit game, played with $5 bets and raises Pre-Flop and on the Flop and $10 bets and raises on the Turn and the River. Spread limit games are ones in which the betting in a given round is constrained to a particular range. So a $1–$4 spread limit game would allow a bet from $1 to $4 on any round. The structure of a game has a substantial impact on appropriate strategy.

Stuck Losing money.

Stud Usually short for Seven-Card Stud. Also refers to Stud games in general, including Five-Card Stud, in which each player is dealt a number of nonshared cards and he must use only those cards.

Suck Out To win a hand by virtue of hitting a very weak draw often with poor pot odds.

Suit Clubs, diamonds, hearts, and spades. Also something they insist men wear in very fancy foreign casinos.

Suited Of the same suit. Also men wearing the right clothing in very fancy foreign casinos.

Sweat To sweat someone is to watch them play from the rail, in order to lend your support.

Table The word "table" can be used to refer to community cards, the poker table itself, or the players at the table as a group. Examples: *When the ace hit the table, I checked. The table was playing loose, so I was bluffing less than usual. This is a nice table. I especially like the tartan finish.*

Table Change If you're playing at a public card room and you'd like to play at a table other than the one you're currently at, you can ask the floor staff for a table change. Various card rooms handle this differently, but typically you'll be moved as soon as an opening develops, and a player from the seating list will be moved into your seat.

Table Cop A player who calls with the intention of keeping other players honest is said to be playing table cop. Also a player who makes an effort to point out violations, often of insignificant casino rules. The latter can be very annoying.

Table Stakes Table stakes is simply the rule that a player may only wager money he has on the table at the beginning of a hand. Almost all poker games are played this way. Usually it also implies that money may not be removed from the table at any time (exceptions are made for tipping), although money may be added to one's stacks between hands. A player who goes all-in at a table-stakes game may not continue to bet and only competes for the main pot. To the best of my knowledge, Maryland is the only place where most of the games are not table stakes. They also talk funny in Maryland.

Table Talk Any discussion at the table of the hand currently under way, especially by players not involved in the pot and especially any talk that might affect play. Depending on the nature of the discussion, table talk is often considered somewhere between rude and an act of war. The most common example of table talk to be avoided is announcing what cards you've folded. In England, table talk may get you banned from the card room. Don't talk about hands unless you are in them, and don't suggest plays during a hand to other players, when you're not in a pot.

Tell A tell is any habit or behavior that gives other players more information about your hand than they would have gotten simply from your play. For instance, you might unconsciously scratch your ear every time you bluff. Or you might notice that another player's hands shake whenever he has a strong hand. The value of tells in the low-limit game is highly overrated. In high-limit poker they may be invaluable.

Texas Hold'em Hey guys, read the book for pity's sake!

Three of a Kind Three cards of the same rank. Also called "trips."

Tight Playing tight simply means playing fewer hands and folding them earlier. A tight table is a table dominated by tight players. Most players at low limits do not play tightly enough, but tight play alone (without suitable aggression) will not make you into a winning player.

Tilt Good poker means disciplined play. However, even good players are often tempted to make dubious plays when they get frustrated, angry, or upset for any reason. They go "on tilt." I knew one player who did it every game. The rest of us would make side bets as to when during the evening he would begin throwing a tantrum. Tilt comes from the world of pinball when players try to tilt the machine to gain an advantage. Typical tilt play is too loose and aggressive because a player on tilt wants very badly to win a pot and isn't rational enough to wait for cards that are worth playing or situations that are worth attacking.

Time Charge   Money collected from each player periodically is called a "time charge," or a "seat charge," and you're said to be "paying time" to play. "Time" is also what you are supposed to say whenever you need more than about a second to decide what to do.

To Go   An amount to go is the amount it takes to enter the pot.

Toke   A tip, usually a tip to the dealer after winning the pot. Tips are usually between $1 and $5, depending on the limit, the size of the pot, and the generosity of the player.

Top Pair   If there are three cards of different ranks on the Flop and you pair the highest one, you have the top pair.

Tournament   The general idea behind poker tournaments is that a bunch of poker players sit down with the same number of chips (tournament chips), and eventually, only one player has any chips left. The order in which players drop out decides who finishes where. In order to ensure that the event will finish in a reasonable time, tournaments institute a schedule by which the blinds increase. Tournaments are usually played with chips that have no value outside the tournament. So a buy-in of $100 might get you $2,000 in tournament chips to play with, but you can't cash them out in the middle. Tournaments are very varied, and you would be wise to read about them in a book that describes strategies and tactics for tournament play before playing in one.

Trips   Three of a kind.

Trey   Threes are sometimes called "treys."

Turn   The fourth of five community cards in Hold'em.

Two Pair   A hand consisting of two cards of one rank and two cards of another rank (and an unpaired card).

Under the Gun   The first player to act after the blinds is said to be under the gun.

Underdog   When two hands face off, the underdog is the one who is less likely to win than the other. Surely you knew that, right?

Up   Aces up is two pair with aces as the higher pair. Kings up is two pair with kings as the higher pair. What do you think queens up is?

Value   Value means the return you get on your investment; the expected increase in your equity in the pot (your return) as compared to the size of your bet or raise (your investment).

Variance   If you have a sufficient advantage at the game you're playing, you expect to make money over the long haul. Variance is the statistical measure of dispersion, or just how widely your results will be distributed. When variance is high enough, a small advantage may be of no use during your lifetime. When variance is low enough, a small sample will be much more likely to reflect your real advantage (or disadvantage). In other words, variance describes just how long the long haul is. In poker terms, high variance means that a small number of hands will not be very representative of your long-term expectation. Variance is such a strong contributor to poker results that it often obscures the importance of good play. The best player at the table may start with the best cards and still have far less than a 50 percent chance of winning the hand. A skilled professional can lose money over days or weeks, without necessarily playing badly. Bad play may be rewarded in the short term. Or as one poker buddy once said to me in exasperation, "Randomness is a bitch, ain't it?"

Variance is what makes losing players think they have a chance in the long run, and what gives them a real chance in the short run. It keeps poor players coming back. Different qualities of the other players at the table can contribute to your overall variance at a given table. If many of the players are maniacs, your variance may be high at that table. On the other hand, exceptionally weak and passive players will reduce your variance. The variance you experience will be affected not just by the nature of the game but also by your style of play and by the styles of those you play against.

Walk To walk in poker is to be away from the table long enough to miss one or more hands. Such people and people who do so frequently are called "walkers." Perhaps in Australian casinos they go on walkabout. Australian players, is this so?

Weak A style of play characterized by readiness to fold and reluctance to raise. Weak is also used generally to describe a poor player or a table that's easy to beat. It has also been used to describe jokes I make at the table. Whoops, there is another one.

Wild Card A card that can serve as any other card in making your hand. Casino poker does not have wild card games.

Index

About the Author

NEIL MYERS was not brought up in a poker-playing household. He didn't learn his poker skills "at his grandpappy's knee" or watching his big brother play. He never played in college dorms or in the navy or in a regular "Thursday Night Game." Instead, he learned by reading poker books, by playing against computer programs, and by honing his skills in low-limit games in Manhattan's semi-legal poker clubs and the poker rooms in Atlantic City. He is a self-made poker creation. Neil discovered that by approaching the game in this way, the learning curve was steep. As a result, he quickly reached a skill level most people only achieved after a decade or two of play. For over three years he has made a comfortable, regular side income playing low-limit games. Today he enjoys visiting casinos where Hold'em is played, confident in the knowledge that he can beat the game, not risk too much money, and have a lot of fun too. Neil believes that if you read, study, and apply the wisdom of this book, you can do the same.

Neil has never had the desire to become a full-time poker professional but instead enjoys the thrill, fun, and steady profit of taking part in cash games and playing the occasional tournament. When he is not playing poker, Neil teaches sales, marketing, and negotiation and acts as an adviser and trainer for companies that want to improve the performance of their sales and marketing staff. He also teaches weapons disarmament to civilians and law enforcement officers. Since he is known as a "happy" player at the tables, he's never had to use these skills in a poker setting! He lives in Yonkers, New York.